FROM SUFFERING TO SURRENDER

From Suffering to Surrender

Transforming Life's Challenges Into Blessings

Ashley Lane Adams

Published by Game Changer Publishing

Paperback ISBN: 978-1-967424-93-1

Hardcover ISBN: 978-1-967424-94-8

Digital ISBN: 978-1-967424-95-5

GC GAME CHANGER
PUBLISHING
www.GameChangerPublishing.com

For my heart treasures, Robert and Elizabeth.
May you experience uninhibited freedom and unstoppable joy
in this lifetime and for all of eternity.

FREE GIFT

A meditation for you to cultivate inner peace!
In gratitude,
Ashley

Scan the QR Code Here:

FROM SUFFERING TO SURRENDER

TRANSFORMING LIFE'S CHALLENGES INTO BLESSINGS

ASHLEY LANE ADAMS

FOREWORD

I was listening to my intuition, and I was taking action that expressed that abuse is not okay and that staying married is not more important than walking away from destructive and unacceptable behavior. For any woman who is in a relationship that is abusive or toxic, you have to listen to yourself and not anyone else around you. If you know in your heart that you need to leave, then that is what you must do.

Such words depicting the hard choices made throughout Ashley's life tell a story of courage. And courage, especially where there is abuse, is sometimes very hard to find. Putting pen to paper, Ashley invites us with heartfelt sensitivity into the complexity of finding this courage and, through her vulnerability, provides hope that when this courage is found and acted on, cycles of abuse may be broken and trauma healed from.

Finding this courage may appear daunting, and changing present circumstances may appear impossible. But when you find the courage to take back your life and step into the light as Ashley has, the impossible kneels before this power, for fear will have lost its grip within your heart.

I am very grateful to have come to know Ashley and witness the power of radical acceptance and the power of transformative thoughts. It is a privilege to see these practices embodied and principles lived out daily with her children and others she interacts with. Her story is a testimony that even though the way forward may be unclear, when we learn to lean in and trust ourselves, the path of peace is an ever-present one.

May this book be a helpmate to look within and respond to the call of courage speaking now.

Matthew Vanderford ~ Co-Founder, lvngck.com

CONTENTS

Dedication   iii

Free Gift   v

Foreword   1

Introduction   5

1. A Brief History   9

2. My Divorce   25

3. Who am I?   33

4. Forgiveness   45

5. The Inner Work   57

6. Acceptance and Surrender   75

7. A Spiritual Path   85

8. Self-Love   95

9. Beliefs About Worthiness and Abundance   105

10. Relationships: Our Best Teachers   115

11. All is Well   125

Conclusion   131

Suggested Reading   133

Thank You For Reading My Book!   135

INTRODUCTION

Beloved, if you are reading this, then this book was meant to find you. It is no accident that you are reading these words at this exact moment in your life. The messages within these covers found their way to you to shed light on questions that your soul has been whispering to you and that you are now ready to hear.

If you're reading this, then I'm willing to bet you have experienced some large-scale disappointment in your life. Maybe, like me, you had plans for your life to go in a certain direction and look a certain way, but something happened, or a series of things happened, and you woke up one day with the painful awareness that your life did not look the way you had wanted it to look.

As a trauma-informed life coach, I work with courageous souls to overcome their self-imposed limitations, to cultivate surrender, and to embody the happiest and most expressed versions of themselves. I was called into this work because of a large-scale life disappointment that took me in a completely different direction than I had expected to go. The event that pulled the carpet out from under my feet was a divorce and being thrust into single motherhood with an infant and a neurodivergent three-year-old.

I didn't know it then, but the Universe had initiated a journey for me that would fundamentally transform the way I experienced myself and my life. My path was not easy or without suffering, but it would eventually teach me to consciously decide who I wanted to be rather than allow myself to be a victim of previously established subconscious patterns. My new knowledge and experience of how to navigate my world would eventually reveal to me how to transform relationships and life situations once dominated by hatred and fear into those ruled by love and acceptance.

My journey has been a deep spiritual quest for truth, and in this continual study and exploration, I have discovered what it takes for me to live more and more in a state of inner peace, trusting in my higher power.

I never imagined that I would be a single mom, doing all the heavy lifting of figuring out how to make a living while raising two children, one of them prone to violent anger outbursts. It has felt frustrating, overwhelming, lonely, and sometimes utterly hopeless, but I realized I could either accept my reality, which created peace, or I could continue to fight against it, which created suffering.

That is what this book is about. It is about my journey and the tools I acquired along the way that have empowered me to move from living in a state of resistance and fear to one of surrender and, ultimately, love for all that is.

In this book, I share parts of my story, as well as the mindset and spiritual tools that have enabled me to set myself free. I share it with you so that you, too, may find peace, regardless of whatever difficulty you are currently experiencing. If it was possible for me, it is possible for you. I know this without a shadow of a doubt.

*Note: I use different words in this book to refer to my understanding of a higher power, including God/Goddess, Universe, Conscious Awareness, and Divine Spirit. Readers may insert whatever name they want to use for their own personal higher power. It is my intention to be inclusive of people of all religious backgrounds and spiritual beliefs.

CHAPTER 1
A BRIEF HISTORY

*"The moment you accept what troubles you've
been given; the door will open."*
—Rumi

I was born into a Southern family in the small town of Oxford, Mississippi, home to the University of Mississippi. When I was one, my family moved to Destin, Florida, known as the world's luckiest fishing village. Destin is located in the Florida Panhandle, which has a very different culture from South Florida because it is largely populated by migrants from other Southern states, such as Mississippi, Alabama, and Georgia. My parents, both Southern transplants, believed in the importance of following many of the Southern cultural norms, such as going to church on Sundays, dressing appropriately, hosting dinner parties, and writing thank-you cards, to name a few.

I was blessed to be raised by parents who always made it clear they loved me, provided very well for my physical and educational needs, and gave me many freedoms to discover who I was. Despite their gallant efforts at being great parents, one of the biggest messages that I internalized as a young girl was that my main responsibilities in life were to look pretty, be nice, and do things in a socially acceptable way. In other words, based on my experiences and the messaging that I received as a little girl from my family, culture, and society, I formulated the belief that my self-worth came from gaining the acceptance of others by being polite, following rules, and being agreeable.

I am also an empath, which means I can intuitively pick up on other people's emotional states. As a child, when a teacher or other authority figure expressed any disappointment in me, it affected me deeply, and I would internalize a profound sense of guilt and shame. Additionally, my brother, who was three years older than me and my only sibling, was very often in trouble. So, I made an unconscious internal decision that I had to be perfect and that it was my job to please everyone. I fell flawlessly into the role of people-pleaser and peacemaker, a role I continued to play for many years until it became clear that not only was it no longer working for me, but that it was actually ruining my life.

While studying abroad in France during my sophomore year of college, I met my first husband, Francis. I had been in a mild depression during my first year away from home, and he was a passionate French musician who completely swept me off my feet in a way that felt like a dream, like a real-life rom-com. He made me feel alive in a way that was totally new to me. Being only twenty years old and making an emotional choice, I dove in headfirst and didn't look back. I had felt so fundamentally disconnected from the people around me for such a long time, and so alone and isolated in the world. In many ways, meeting Francis felt like a lifeboat. It was the first time that I can remember as a young woman that I felt deeply connected, seen, understood, and adored by another human. It was like nothing I had ever experienced before.

Lesson: When you are not in a place of wholeness within yourself, you are not in a healthy place to start a relationship because you will be attracting your partner from a place of lack— wanting him or her to fill the emptiness that you feel within yourself. You must find love and contentment from within yourself first, and from that place, you will be able to attract a healthy partner.

From where I sit now, I can see Francis utilized a lot of emotional manipulation in our relationship. I can see how I was love-bombed at the beginning of our relationship. In my case, he pushed me to go very deep very quickly, talking about our future when we'd only hung out a few times. Francis quickly became controlling and, at times, forceful, pushing for the things he wanted and becoming angry and inflexible when I did not want the same things. However, because I was twenty years old, a people-pleaser, and I had an extremely strong desire to cling to the most real and deepest connection I had ever experienced, I tried with all of my power to make the relationship work. I believed that the kind of connection that I had with him was a once-in-a-lifetime thing, so I just had to accept all the negatives that came along with it.

Lesson #1: There is no need to rush things in love. If he/she is the right person, he/she will not go anywhere but will allow things to unfold organically over time.

Lesson #2: A healthy relationship does not have any toxicity in it, and you do not have to endure unhealthy/destructive behavior to experience the good.

Francis and I got married so that he could live in the U.S. with me, and we moved to Topanga, California, a small community outside of Los Angeles. Our partnership had turned into an open relationship, meaning that we were open to being with other people while remaining in our marriage. Looking back, I believe that the reason I was willing to be in an open relationship was because I knew deep down that Francis was not the right person for me. I knew in my heart that there was someone better out there for me. This was the place I was in when I met my second husband, Chris, who has become the biggest part of my story to date because he is the father of my beloved children.

Francis and I got the quickest and easiest divorce in history since there were no children or finances involved, and I jumped straight into my relationship with Chris without missing a beat. At that point, I was in a very insecure place in my life. I was pursuing acting in Los Angeles, which, in my case, meant I was working in a very toxic restaurant environment and constantly feeling the gap between where I was and where I wanted to be. I had a deep desire to be successful and an enormous feeling of helplessness in terms of how to actually achieve that success. I was desperate to feel as if my life was finally coming together and making sense. After having known for some time that things weren't right with Francis, I wanted to feel like I had finally made the right choice, and even though I was pursuing acting, what I longed for on a deeper level was to get married and have children. I was thirty-one at that point, and I could feel my biological clock ticking.

Lesson: *The biggest reason that you should not jump out of one relationship and directly into another is because it doesn't allow you the time to be alone with yourself to learn who you are, independent of someone else. This time alone is crucial for you to learn to love and fully accept yourself. Until you are able to be content with yourself and deeply know yourself, you can't really know what kind of partner you desire. Rather, you will just jump into another relationship from a place of subconscious patterning and from a desire to fill a void.*

Chris and I quickly moved in together, and after a few years, we began to talk about marriage. Since my marriage to Francis had not been a success, I was extremely afraid of making another mistake. I did not trust my own judgment. I had felt so sure about Francis, and I had been so wrong. I reached out to my mom, consulted my best friend, and prayed fervently to God, seeking assurance I was getting it right this time.

There had been some things in the very beginning that had made me feel uncomfortable with Chris, the largest of which was that he had a quick temper that made me feel nervous. I was aware that I didn't like that, but I chose to overlook it in the hope that the anger I had seen was only linked to a few isolated events or that he would grow out of it. I really didn't want to look at it because I was too attached to the idea of finally getting it right and settling down and starting a family—two things that I felt would give me a sense of safety and belonging in the world. So I decided to go for it. We began planning our wedding and moved to Florida, where my family lived and where Chris would pursue real estate and we could start our family.

Lesson: Be conscientious about listening to any inner whisperings that you experience early in a relationship that tell you when something is off, no matter how small or insignificant they may seem. These inner whisperings are your inner guidance system informing you of your inner truth.

There were so many things about how Chris showed up at our wedding and honeymoon that hurt my heart. There was an overall feeling that he wasn't on my team. I struggled for a long time, trying to understand why my wedding felt like more of a negative memory than a positive one. Ultimately, it wasn't until we had our first child that I realized there was something very, very wrong... something that would possibly make our marriage unsustainable for me.

Soon after our first child, Robert, was born, I sat down to dinner with Chris, and Robert began to cry, as babies do. Chris became enraged. He was furious that we couldn't sit down to a peaceful dinner as we had done before having a baby. Chris couldn't wrap his head around this change. I started noticing more and more things like this—his resistance to and anger about many of the typical changes that occur in people's lives when they have a child. He would become enraged when Robert woke in the night or when he got sick and threw up. As Robert got older, Chris would rage about him tracking sand on the floor after playing outside or dropping food on the floor when he ate. I didn't notice it all at once because it unfolded slowly over time. All I knew was that I had begun to walk on eggshells to keep Chris from exploding into a rage. It had gotten to the point that if he was around, I was in a constant state of hyper-awareness and fear.

Lesson: It is often difficult to see toxic patterns in our own intimate relationships because the severity of the behavior often starts off mild and then gradually intensifies over time.

Two particular things happened that jolted me out of the cycle that I had felt stuck in: a particularly awful night in which Chris became physical with me and a podcast episode that opened up my eyes to the truth of what I was experiencing. I had endured the anger outbursts, yelling, name-calling, and teasing that brought me to tears, along with the absolute disregard for the validity of my emotions. But one night, I found myself backed up against a wall, Chris's hand on my throat, while I held three-year-old Robert in my arms and Elizabeth listened from the next room.

Earlier that night, Chris had texted me to tell me that he would be home soon and that he planned to put a pizza in the oven for us. I ended up having a few extra minutes in between doing things for the kids, so I went ahead and put the pizza in the oven so it would be ready when he got home. When Chris arrived, though, he was extremely angry that I had not waited for him to put the pizza in the oven. He was additionally frustrated because Robert was running around making noise, as three-year-olds do. Chris began raging at both of us and would not let up. I immediately went into fight-or-flight mode—I had decided I would call my mom in these situations and have her come over. When I got my phone, this angered Chris as well, and he grabbed my phone from me and would not give it back.

Now he was even more angry and his yelling intensified further. Elizabeth was secure and fine in her baby seat, so I picked Robert up and walked toward the front door to go for a little walk to escape the verbal attack, but Chris walked swiftly in front of us and blocked me from leaving. At that point, I started to scream for him to let me leave. This is when he put his hand on my throat and backed me up against the wall while Robert observed the entire scene from my arms.

An eerie calm came over me. I knew that the only way to get Chris to calm down was to *pretend* I was calm and that everything was okay, so I did. The moment that he de-escalated and went to change out of his work clothes, I ran next door and asked my neighbor to come over for a little while. She knew immediately from the look on my face that something was gravely wrong, so she came right away without question. She sat with us at dinner for a little while, and when she could see that all was calm again, she returned home. We went through our bedtime routine as usual, which was the only way I could manage to arrange for someone from my family to come help me without Chris suspecting anything. I knew that he would not have let me leave on my own with the kids. I needed backup.

I had texted SOS to my parents and brother. My parents were at a party that night and away from their phones, but after my kids were in bed, my brother came over to escort me and the kids to his house for the night. Chris did not fight us leaving because he knew he would have to deal with my brother, and he was only scary and intimidating when others weren't around. I had to wake my babies up from a sound sleep, and I will never forget the long, dark ride on Highway 98 to my brother's house, Robert looking scared and confused, and my baby girl crying the whole way.

Had I known then what I know now, I would have filed for divorce the following day as well as pressed charges against him for what he did, but when we are in the midst of this type of trauma, we often cannot see clearly. All we can do is our best at that moment to survive. Often, it takes us getting out of the storm and looking back to be able to gain insight into what truly happened. In my case, a report was never made, and when I did end up filing for divorce, my attorney said that there was simply no way to prove what had happened. In court, it would have come down to a *"he said, she said"* because there had been no witnesses. So, according to the official record, it's as if it never happened.

When Chris put his hand on my throat, something inside of me broke and was never the same again. I knew at the deepest level that I would never trust him again, and all the love I had ever felt for him was completely gone. I was totally empty. So, I was primed to hear the message that came to me in the form of a podcast a few months later. The speaker, who was the head of a women's shelter in Texas, said that knowing if you are experiencing abuse in an intimate relationship is very simple. All you need to do is ask yourself one question: Are you fearful of your partner? It is that simple. The moment I heard that, a lightbulb went off. An internal voice definitively said, *Yes, I am fearful of my partner.* I had been living in constant fear of him getting angry at me, Robert, or our new baby girl, Elizabeth. He yelled in such an intense and violent way—it made my entire body go into fight or flight to the point that my brain would shut down, and I couldn't even formulate coherent sentences. (This is a normal biological reaction to fear.)

Lesson: *You should never feel fearful of your partner. If you experience fear in your relationship, you are in an abusive dynamic.*

Up until that point in my life, I didn't realize that there even were such things as covert or emotional abuse. They are both concepts that, until fairly recently, haven't been widely known or discussed. Once I discovered this, I began an intensive online study about them. I had finally found an explanation for why I had been feeling the way I had with Chris! It was such a relief to know I wasn't crazy, and I could make a choice to no longer accept that kind of behavior in my life. I didn't have to live in fear anymore! Hallelujah!

Note: I developed Bell's palsy near the end of my marriage. The right side of my face was paralyzed for about a week. Though I have no way of proving this, I believe that I developed this condition because of the level of stress that I had been living under.

What I learned from my research was that covert, which means hidden, and emotional abuse are, in some cases, more dangerous in the long term than physical abuse. The reason for this is that these types of abuse actually break down your immune system. Someone who experiences covert abuse over a long period of time will experience their body breaking down from the inside out as well as their mind breaking down. Whereas in a physical abuse scenario, someone might get a black eye or bruise, which is outwardly visible, with emotional abuse, you don't see an outward mark on the body. Instead, over time, people's bodies formulate diseases due to the levels of stress that they have been living under. However, since the effects of emotional abuse are not outwardly seen, they are not acknowledged by onlookers, the medical community or the court system, and often not even acknowledged by the people experiencing them.

Lesson: Covert (hidden) abuse and emotional abuse are just as serious, and sometimes even more serious than physical abuse, even though they are very difficult to see.

With my newfound awareness, I started talking to women in my community. I was shocked to realize there were countless women who'd experienced this type of behavior in their relationships, and many of them were living under the false notion that was just how it was. I became passionate about being a voice for women. I wanted people to know that no one deserves to live in fear. In a healthy relationship, there is no fear. I'm not saying that healthy relationships are always easy and without difficulty. Clearly, that's not true, but feeling fearful of your partner is not normal in the context of a healthy relationship.

Despite my passion for this, I remained deeply concerned about how my divorce would affect my kids, so I studied a great deal about this as well. What I concluded was that the challenges and struggles that my children would face from being in a divorced family were much less than the pain and suffering that they would experience if I were to have stayed with their dad. I didn't want to teach my children it was okay to stay in a relationship in which someone treats you poorly.

If I stayed in the marriage, I would have taught my daughter that it was okay to accept emotional abuse, and my son would have learned it was okay to treat women in emotionally abusive ways. Additionally, my children would not have lived in an environment of joy, peace, and freedom. When I was married to their dad, I was not joyful, and I was not free to be myself. I was under constant stress, and I was not at peace. By leaving, I became a happier, more peaceful human and, therefore, a better mother.

Lesson: *You are not doing your children a favor by staying in a toxic marriage for their sake. Rather, you are teaching them to model toxic relationships in their own lives.*

Soon Chris moved out, and I found myself living in our marital home alone with my kids. It was through creating this physical distance from Chris, this space away from him, that I was able to start seeing how much of myself I had lost in the marriage and the real degree to which I had been living in fear. By getting back into my own space, I could feel my nervous system begin to relax again. I finally felt safe and free to be myself again.

Lesson: Creating physical distance with someone is so important in order to be able to get back in touch with who you really are when you have been intertwined with someone. It is imperative to create space away from them so you can start relearning who you are on your own.

Now that I had all of this time and space to myself, or as much as you can have when you're raising a baby and a three-year-old, I started to look back to try to understand how I had allowed myself to get into such an unhealthy relationship. From my new vantage point, I could see how often things in the relationship had simply felt wrong, but instead of listening to my body, I'd allowed my mind to overrule.

Lesson: To live in alignment with your truth, you must be in tune with your body's intuition, i.e., the way your body communicates to you through your feelings. Our bodies never lie, but our minds can tell us all kinds of false stories.

I remembered one of my first dates with Chris. We had gone out for sushi, and his sushi ended up coming out before mine. He became highly frustrated to the point that it changed the entire energy of our date. He couldn't get over the fact that he had his sushi, and I didn't have mine, even though I wasn't worried about it. He was rude to the waiter, and the overall feeling at the table was horrible. This memory may seem like a small thing, but it was reflective of the way that he navigates disappointment.

I'd felt extremely uneasy in my body that night. I had a tightness in my stomach, and I felt nervous. I felt uncomfortable, like I couldn't trust him. It was moments like this, multiplied by a thousand, that I began to remember as I looked back.

Another thing I remembered vividly was a time when we had gone to visit his sister and her two children. Her little boy was infatuated with Chris and followed him around quite a bit. Chris became so frustrated that he got out of the car and slammed the door in a fit of rage in front of the little boy. I didn't understand what had happened, but I now realize this behavior was a red flag. It was a foreshadowing of how he would later parent his own children. As I realized this, I was overcome with guilt and shame that I had not seen all of these red flags at the time.

Lesson: How your partner treats children in his life is how he will parent your future children, and how he reacts under stress in small situations is an indicator of how he will react to larger stressors down the road.

If you are in a relationship that doesn't feel right, there is a reason for that, and you are not crazy to feel that way. You can trust how your body feels, and you deserve to be in a relationship in which your partner is *for you*. Beginning to listen to your body and trust it is one of the most powerful things you can do.

Lesson: Your body's feelings and sensations are always a direct manifestation of your inner truth.

CHAPTER ONE LESSONS:

- When you are not in a place of wholeness within yourself, you are not in a healthy place to start a relationship because you will be attracting your partner from a place of lack—wanting him or her to fill the emptiness that you feel within yourself. You must find love and contentment from within yourself first, and from that place, you will be able to attract a healthy partner.

- There is no need to rush things in love. If he/she is the right person, he/she will not go anywhere but will allow things to unfold organically over time.

- A healthy relationship does not have any toxicity in it, and you do not have to endure unhealthy/destructive behavior to experience the good.

- The biggest reason that you should not jump out of one relationship and directly into another is because it doesn't allow you the time to be alone with yourself to learn who you are, independent of someone else. This time alone is crucial for you to learn to love and fully accept yourself. Until you are able to be content with yourself and deeply know yourself, you can't really know what kind of partner you desire. Rather, you will just jump into another relationship from a place of subconscious patterning and from a desire to fill a void.

- Be conscientious about listening to any inner whisperings that you experience early in a relationship that tell you when something is off, no matter how small or insignificant they may seem. These inner whisperings are your inner guidance system informing you of your inner truth.

- It is often difficult to see toxic patterns in our own intimate relationships because the severity of the behavior often starts off mild and then gradually intensifies over time.

- You should never feel fearful of your partner. If you experience fear in your relationship, you are in an abusive dynamic.

- Covert (hidden) abuse and emotional abuse are just as serious, and sometimes even more serious than physical abuse, even though they are very difficult to see.

- You are not doing your children a favor by staying in a toxic marriage for their sake. Rather, you are teaching them to model toxic relationships in their own lives.

- Creating physical distance with someone is so important in order to be able to get back in touch with who you really are when you have been intertwined with someone. It is imperative to create space away from them so you can start relearning who you are on your own.

- To live in alignment with your truth, you must be in tune with your body's intuition, i.e., the way your body communicates to you through your feelings. Our bodies never lie, but our minds can tell us all kinds of false stories.

- How your partner treats children in his life is how he will parent your future children, and how he reacts under stress in small situations is an indicator of how he will react to larger stressors down the road.

- Your body's feelings and sensations are always a direct manifestation of your inner truth.

Note: *If you feel you may be in an emotional or covert abuse dynamic, please visit themendproject.com to empower yourself with the knowledge you need to understand the patterns of the abuse.*

CHAPTER 2
MY DIVORCE

"All human actions are motivated at their deepest level by
two emotions—fear or love. In truth there are only two emotions—
only two words in the language of the soul... Fear wraps our bodies
in clothing, love allows us to stand naked. Fear clings to and clutches
all that we have, love gives all that we have away. Fear holds close,
love holds dear. Fear grasps, love lets go. Fear rankles,
love soothes. Fear attacks, love amends."
——Neale Donald Walsch,
Conversations with God: An Uncommon Dialogue, Book 1

As I was navigating my divorce process and researching covert abuse, I was committed to getting full custody of my kids and only allowing Chris to have supervised visitations. I believed that his emotional and verbal abuse would have devastating effects on the formulation of my kids' personalities and the way that they learned to relate to other people, but I soon learned from many conversations with attorneys that full custody was not going to be a possibility because I did not have hard proof of the abuse that had occurred.

Each milestone I reached during the divorce process required letting go of another expectation regarding custody. In the end, we settled with me having slightly more than fifty percent custody. I could have gone to court to fight this, but after much deliberation, confusion, and heartache, I chose not to because my lawyer advised I was likely to come out with exactly fifty percent custody, not to mention the finances that would be necessary and the enormous emotional toll that it would take.

I was terrified of going to trial with Chris. I had read multiple accounts about how narcissistic men fared better in the court system than protective mothers did because of their confidence and charisma. Chris is a very intelligent man and presents himself very well. I had no idea what he would do or say. He had already threatened to say I was an abusive mother and mentally ill. When he said these things to me, I was fear-struck, realizing he would be willing to take any route possible in an effort to get what he wanted, including blatantly lying.

I was so anxious about going to trial that I had multiple nightmares in which Chris attempted to strangle me in the courtroom or tried to hit me in the parking lot with his car. Clearly, I was in an intense state of fear. It also didn't help that I was reading stories about abusive fathers who murdered their own children to get back at their wives. There are many statistics about how the most dangerous time for women in abusive cycles is when they choose to leave their partners because the partners can't deal with the fact that they no longer have control. Essentially, as I went further down the rabbit hole of research, I got more and more scared. Instead of surrendering to what was in front of me and trusting that the Universe would guide me and my children to where we were meant to be, my mind was consumed with worst-case scenarios.

Lesson: *When we put our focus on our fears and remain in resistance to the reality that is unfolding in front of us, we create massive suffering for ourselves. Conversely, when we lean into the knowing that the Universe is leading us to exactly where we are supposed to be, we can trust and surrender to what is. This is what allows us to access peace, no matter what is happening in our lives.*

Every time I talked to Chris, it was extremely tense, uncomfortable, and anxiety-inducing. There was a lot of animosity and hatred between us. In one phone call, he said he and his attorney were seeking full custody. I don't even remember how he justified this, as I was so consumed by shock, rage, and absolute terror. I couldn't believe that he would actually try to take my children away from me completely! Had I been in a rational state, I would have seen he could not achieve this, but he was speaking into my deepest, darkest fear, and it worked because I buckled and offered him a new custody proposal that I would not have had I been calm and grounded. I had been emotionally manipulated again, and I had been completely unaware of it.

Lesson: *Decisions made from a space of fear will never be in alignment with your highest desire.*

At that time, I needed someone to say, "Whatever you do, DO NOT talk to him about anything concerning the divorce or the settlement! He is using subtle scare tactics and strategies to manipulate you into getting what he wants." For years, I beat myself up over that conversation. I felt a tangible pain in my heart over it. I believed that it was because of this moment of fear and emotional manipulation that he ended up receiving more custody than he likely would have had I not engaged with him. It would have served me much better to just allow the process to unfold organically and trust that it was all in the hands of my higher power.

Lesson: *Only harm can come from going over and over past events that you wish had happened differently. In order to experience peace, you have to let these things go and trust that there is meaning and purpose in how everything unfolds for you.*

After talking it over with many people and going over every angle that I could think of with my attorney, I agreed to what Chris and his attorney had offered rather than going to trial. The uncertainty of what would come from going to trial, my terror of what Chris would be willing to do, and the financial burden that it was putting on my family all had me arrive at the conclusion that accepting the settlement agreement was my best option. At the time, though, I did not feel at peace about it.

I had been anxious for it to all be finished so that I could get my life back on track. I wanted to stop waking up every night with anxiety and scary visions of losing my children. It had been all-consuming, and all I could think about outside of taking care of my kids. I felt like my life was utterly on hold. At that time, I had no spiritual practice, and I had very little social support. My parents were there for me, but for the most part, I felt isolated and alone. I was ready to rebuild my life.

The day that we signed the divorce papers, I felt a combination of relief and remorse—relief that it was over and remorse that the outcome was not at all what I had desired it to be. Had I sold out on my kids? Had I taken the easy way out? Did I take the path of fear rather than the path of faith? On top of all of this, my attorney advised that we not mention the abuse in any of the divorce documentation because of the lack of proof and because it wouldn't change the outcome of the settlement. This made it seem as if the abuse had never occurred, which was a lie. It felt like there was no validation for what my kids and I had been through.

What I didn't have the foresight to see at that time was that because the abuse wasn't mentioned in the divorce, it was not something that could be referenced down the line. Once a divorce case is closed, whatever is in the documentation is considered fact in the eyes of the court. In other words, because the abuse had not been mentioned in the divorce settlement, it could never again be mentioned in future custody proceedings regarding my children. So by choosing not to include it in the official marital dissolution settlement, it was as if the abuse had been erased from history.

The night after I signed the settlement, I lay in bed next to my son, Robert, unable to sleep. I thought I would feel better once everything was finalized, but I felt empty and afraid I had made a mistake. I lay there, unable to sleep, feeling sick to my stomach and aching all over. I wanted to feel a sense of completion or healing, but I didn't. I soon realized that even though I was no longer married to Chris, our lives were still entangled, especially when it came to the kids. In many ways, this was when some of the more complex and subtle challenges would arise in regard to the realities of sharing custody with him.

During this chapter of my life, I had so much anxiety, and I rarely felt any joy or peace. I was navigating life without a spiritual compass, with no answers about why things were unfolding the way they were, and with no certainty as to what was ahead. It was scary and uncomfortable, and all I could do was move forward day by day and trust that the answers would present themselves eventually, but it was a very dark chapter in which I felt very alone.

This was not my first dark chapter, and it would not be my last, but what I possess now that I did not at that time is the certainty that the Universe is unfolding events in my life exactly as they are meant to be for my highest good and for the highest good of all. Equipped with this belief, no matter what happens in my life, I am able to surrender to the Divine's plan for me and trust that it is taking me somewhere that my heart longs to be. This belief doesn't mean that life always feels easy, and sometimes I still struggle with understanding the purpose of human suffering, but knowing that the Universe is ultimately in control and has my highest interest at heart is a great comfort in times of pain and confusion.

Lesson: We all go through dark chapters in our lives. It is part of the human experience. But it is our faith in our higher power and our ability to surrender to that greater force that will empower us to traverse these chapters with ease, grace, peace, and even certain shades of joy.

Living our lives without faith is painful. It is lonely and sometimes downright hopeless. When we can adopt the belief that the Universe is for us and that it is orchestrating our lives in perfect accordance with Divine Order, we move from a place of feeling like victims in a seemingly random and cruel world to a place of knowing that, in the end, all is as it is meant to be and we will only truly understand it all when we transition into life after death.

Lesson: When navigating our darkest moments in life, the only way that I have found to access peace is to surrender, to let go and choose to trust that everything is unfolding in divine perfection according to the will of God/Goddess/Universe, and that ultimately, it is for the highest good of all.

CHAPTER TWO LESSONS:

- When we put our focus on our fears and remain in resistance to the reality that is unfolding in front of us, we create massive suffering for ourselves. Conversely, when we lean into the knowing that the Universe is leading us to exactly where we are supposed to be, we can trust and surrender to what is. This allows us to access peace, no matter what is happening in our lives.

- Decisions made from a space of fear will never be in alignment with your highest desire.

- Only harm can come from going over and over past events that you wish had happened differently. In order to experience peace, you have to let these things go and trust that there is meaning and purpose in how everything unfolds for you.

- We all go through dark chapters in our lives. It is part of the human experience. But it is our faith in our higher power and our ability to surrender to that greater force that will empower us to traverse these chapters with ease, grace, peace, and even certain shades of joy.

- When navigating our darkest moments in life, the only way that I have found to access peace is to surrender; to let go and choose to trust that everything is unfolding in divine perfection according to the will of God/Goddess/Universe, and that ultimately, it is for the highest good of all.

CHAPTER 3
WHO AM I?

"True freedom has to do with the human spirit.
It is the freedom to be who we really are."
—Don Miguel Ruiz,
The Four Agreements.

The more time I had away from my marriage to be alone with my kids, the more I could unravel what had happened in my relationship with Chris. I began to realize the enormity of the stress that I had been living under for years. Now, without that stress, I felt a new spaciousness and freedom. I was relearning how to live in a world in which I didn't have to feel nervous all the time. I didn't have to question myself if I wanted to hang a picture or leave a bowl on the kitchen counter. I didn't have to worry when my kids played in the yard and came inside with grass on their shoes. I could let my kids paint on the kitchen counter! Essentially, I felt free, and it was absolutely liberating!

Life still felt complex and difficult, but the freedom that I felt to just be me, to just be peaceful in my own space with my kids, was worth all the worry and stress that went with getting a divorce, starting a new life, and coming to terms with being a single mom.

In the beginning, I was extremely self-critical. I judged myself heavily for the life decisions that I had made up until that point. I asked myself a lot of disempowering questions, such as, *How could I have gotten it so wrong? How could I have made such a horrible mistake in choosing Chris?* and *Why didn't I go to law school instead of playing the drums and pursuing acting, so I could actually support myself now?* I was forced to face off with the fact that, on top of mothering my babies, I was now the primary breadwinner, and I needed to create a career from scratch to support us, which felt extremely daunting.

Even as I was feeling like a failure, there were also these parts of me that were coming back to life. I felt a new wave of creativity come alive within me and a curiosity about what was now possible for me. Less than a year before, I had felt a sense of dread. I had been in a marriage in which I didn't feel seen, connected, or free to be myself. Now, I knew that real love was possible for me again. The future could hold a relationship in which I could be happy and free and in which I could support and be supported by a partner in a healthy way.

Parts of me that had been lying dormant for many years began to slowly come back online. They were the fundamental parts of me that had always been there that I had buried deep within me. I had hidden them in order to survive my life and my relationships in a way that felt safe to me. I felt that inner expressive part of me knocking on the door and beginning to playfully peek through to see the light. I noticed myself singing out loud again and laughing more with Robert and Elizabeth. I could actually take pleasure in my children and not have to second-guess all of my decisions out of fear of being verbally attacked.

Lesson: You will hide parts of yourself away in certain life situations and relationships when you don't feel safe to express them. Not until you give yourself permission to walk away from the unhealthy situations and free yourself will they re-emerge from within you. (Don't worry, they are never lost! They are always there waiting on you to allow them the freedom and safety to be expressed!)

I realized that the longer I had been in the relationships with Francis and Chris, the more I had lost myself and allowed my voice to be silenced. To keep myself safe and to keep myself from being on the receiving end of anger, criticism, and mean-spirited sarcasm, I simply stopped showing up authentically. I stopped setting boundaries and stopped speaking up when I was uncomfortable or disagreed with something. I stopped expressing my opinions because it was just easier that way, and in doing so, I almost completely lost sight of who I really was.

The week before I left Chris, when I had the certainty that I was going to leave but was still getting my plan together, I went through the motions with him like a robot. It was like doing life on autopilot, with no soul. I felt like a *Stepford Wife*. At the end of that week, Chris commented about what a wonderful week we had had and how well things were going. It was mind-blowing.

In that moment, I realized on a profound level that Chris didn't even see the real me. I had been intentionally agreeing with everything he had said, expressing zero opinions and not showing up authentically all week, and he hadn't even noticed that the real me wasn't there.

After I spent a good deal of time researching covert abuse, emotional abuse, and the overall patterns of abuse, my focus shifted toward asking spiritual questions and searching for answers about what I believed. I was trying to make sense of my life and everything that had happened. I took a deep dive into searching for the truth, searching for *my* truth, independent of anyone else's opinions.

I was soon led to an emotional intelligence and leadership training called *Ascension Leadership Academy* in Austin, Texas. It was an absolutely mind-blowing and life-altering experience. It afforded me the opportunity to see how others experienced me, and I was shocked by what I discovered.

What I learned from the training was that I had been showing up to the world as a doormat, as a person who allows others to walk all over her. I had been showing up as a person who hides, as a person who doesn't believe that she's worthy of having a voice, and as a person who believes that she's less than other people. One thing that I knew for certain was that I didn't want to be *that* person anymore.

Lesson: *You have the power to decide the type of person that you want to be and consciously become that version of yourself.*

The training allowed me to reignite my inner strength, my inner spark, and to reconnect with the truest essence of who I am—the unique expression of Goddess that I came to this planet to be. It forged a passion within me to be a leader, to be more courageous, and it reignited my wild and expressive side. I felt an even deeper calling to help women who were stuck in the place where I had been stuck for so many years, and it was at that point that I became aware of my calling to become a life coach.

What I learned about the person that I had become—the doormat, the person who hides in the background, the people pleaser—was that it was a persona I had created for myself as a child to feel safe as I navigated my young life experiences. It's what we all do. It stemmed from when I had been a peacekeeper in my family of origin.

Now that I understood this, I could consciously choose to be different. I could choose to be whoever I wanted to be, and I could create whatever type of life that I desired to create for myself. My life no longer had to be dictated by my past or by my desire to fulfill other people's expectations for me.

Lesson: You get to choose who you want to be in the world. Who you are does not have to be dictated by your past or by other people's desires for or opinions about you.

I learned that we all create labels for ourselves early on in our childhood development—definitions of who we believe ourselves to be. In my case, I would say things like, *I'm a shy person*, or *I just like to keep my thoughts to myself*. We create these false beliefs to cope with our lives—to feel safe with our realities. We take on these identities in an effort to create security, control, and approval. They aid us in navigating our childhood experiences, but once we reach adulthood, more often than not, these beliefs become self-imposed limitations.

They are not the truth about who we are. Rather, they are false definitions about ourselves that we have believed up until that point. Once we become aware that they are only beliefs and not the truth, we have the power to change them. I had the opportunity to ask myself, *Do I want to be a person who doesn't speak up for herself out of fear, or would I rather be someone who has the courage to speak her truth?* My answer: *I want to have the confidence to speak my truth in the world without fear.*

Lesson: *We all take on certain roles in our childhoods as coping mechanisms to keep ourselves safe. Once we identify them for what they are—beliefs—we become empowered to make a different choice that is in alignment with who we desire to be rather than who we believed we had to be to feel safe.*

Before I cultivated this new awareness, I operated from the belief that what other people said mattered more than what I had to say. I believed that other people were smarter/better than me or more qualified, and therefore, it made sense to defer to them to make decisions for me. After all, they knew better, right? Well, actually... no.

Lesson: *No one knows what is best for you better than you because only you have your own private direct line of communication with the divine within you, and this is the only truth that matters. All the rest can fade into the background if you but let it.*

You never know what seemingly insignificant event in your life can have a profound effect on what you believe about yourself. One life event that led me to believe that I was *less than* happened in high school when I received my SAT and ACT scores. Even though my scores were very good compared to national averages, my two closest friends scored much higher than me. I wasn't aware of it at the time, but on a subconscious level, I formulated the belief that I wasn't as smart as my peers. I remember crying on my bed as my mom did her best to convince me that it wasn't a big deal. As she spoke her words of comfort and encouragement, I heard them, but I didn't believe them. I had already made the inner decision that I was *less than.*

Lesson: The beliefs that we formulate about ourselves happen on an unconscious level and can often be the result of very subtle, seemingly unimportant life events.

One way to refer to these self-imposed limiting beliefs is as our *false selves*. The first step in order to dis-identify with these false selves and to feel safe in the world without them is simply to become aware of them. We first have to be able to clearly identify the beliefs before we are able to consciously decide to change them. From a place of awareness, we can ask ourselves if the belief is supporting us to be, do, and have what we desire or if we would rather create another belief that will support us in cultivating the life and expression of self that feels authentic and in true alignment. We have the power to choose who we want to be rather than to be dictated by subconscious beliefs that we created in our childhoods before we even knew that we were creating them.

Lesson: The more you become aware of the self-limiting beliefs that have been running your life subconsciously, the more you can consciously choose exactly who you want to be and what you want to create in the world.

A practice that I began to let go of my false selves and to bring me back into alignment with my authentic self was re-learning how to listen to my inner voice, my intuition.

"The voice within is the loudest voice. It is the voice which tells you whether everything else is true or false, right or wrong, good or bad. It is the radar that sets the course, steers the ship, guides the journey, if you but let it."
—Neale Donald Walsch,
Conversations with God: An Uncommon Dialogue, Book 1

I realized that what had happened in my relationship with Chris and with so many others was that I would have a tightness in my chest or stomach accompanied by a feeling that something wasn't right. The problem was, instead of listening to that inner whisper, I would allow my mind to override it by rationalizing it away. By not listening to what my inner voice said, I was selling out on myself again and again and losing trust in my ability to take care of myself.

I also began to see that instead of listening to my own inner wisdom, I was outsourcing my decision-making to teachers, parents, pastors, friends, and partners. If there was something that I felt unclear about, the first thing I would do would be to reach out to other people and ask for their opinion. Now, when I feel that urge within myself to ask someone else what to do, I take that uncertainty into a meditation and see what truth/knowing comes up within me. The answer is not always immediate, but it always comes.

Lesson #1: Some people call that inner voice God/Goddess. Others refer to it as the highest self, intuition, or spirit. However you define it, your inner guidance system is always your direct access to the truth.

Lesson #2: *No one outside of you can know your truth, and no one else can tell you your truth. Only you can know your truth, and this knowing can only come from within yourself.*

In the very simplest of terms, for so many years, I had not trusted myself on the most basic level, and I had not listened to the way that my body communicated with me. The difference now was that I was aware of it, and awareness is where it all starts! So I began my journey to relearn who I was at my core and how to trust my body's innate wisdom, my intuition.

CHAPTER THREE LESSONS:

- You will hide parts of yourself away in certain life situations and relationships when you don't feel safe to express them. Not until you give yourself permission to walk away from the unhealthy situations and free yourself will they re-emerge from within you. (Don't worry, they are never lost! They are always there waiting on you to allow them the freedom and safety to be expressed!)

- We all take on certain roles in our childhoods as coping mechanisms to keep ourselves safe. Once we identify them for what they are—beliefs—we become empowered to make a different choice that aligns with who we truly desire to be.

- You have the power to decide the type of person that you want to be and consciously become that version of yourself.

- You get to choose who you want to be in the world. Who you are does not have to be dictated by your past or by other people's desires for or opinions about you.

- We all take on certain roles in our childhoods as coping mechanisms to keep ourselves safe. Once we identify them for what they are—beliefs—we become empowered to make a different choice that is in alignment with who we desire to be rather than who we believed we had to be to feel safe.

- No one knows what is best for you better than you because only you have your own private direct line of communication with the divine within you, and this is the only truth that matters. All the rest can fade into the background if you but let it.

- The beliefs that we formulate about ourselves happen on an unconscious level and can often be the result of very subtle, seemingly unimportant life events.

- The more you become aware of the self-limiting beliefs that have been running your life subconsciously, the more you can consciously choose exactly who you want to be and what you want to create in the world.

- Some people call that inner voice God/Goddess. Others refer to it as the highest self, intuition, or spirit. However you define it, your inner guidance system is always your direct access to the truth.

- No one outside of you can know your truth, and no one else can tell you your truth. Only you can know your truth, and this knowing can only come from within yourself.

CHAPTER 4
FORGIVENESS

"The practice of forgiveness is our most important
contribution to the healing of the world."
—Marianne Williamson,
A Return to Love: Reflections on the Principles of A Course in Miracles

One of the most priceless lessons that I have learned, not only through my divorce but in all of the challenges I've navigated post-divorce, is how hatred is a detriment to a healthy, happy life and how important forgiveness is. It's really easy to lean into hatred when you feel someone has caused you a great deal of harm, and it's even easier to lean into hatred when you feel that someone has caused or is causing harm to your children.

When Robert was around two-and-a-half years old and I was roughly five months pregnant with Elizabeth, I was sitting on the floor changing Robert's diaper, and Chris was sitting right next to us. Robert had become very resistant to having his diaper changed, and he kept kicking and flailing as I was trying to get his diaper on. In one of Robert's attempts to escape, he accidentally kicked me in my pregnant belly, which had me scoot back in pain and frustration. Then, as Robert was waving his arms, he hit Chris in the face. Chris angrily reacted by back-slapping Robert in the face. I remember watching, in what seemed like slow motion, as Robert's face went from shock to turning bright red as his eyes filled with tears.

At first, I was in shock too, but quickly the shock turned into rage, disgust, and downright hatred toward Chris. I scooped Robert up to take him downstairs and comfort him. I had to physically get away from Chris at that moment. Later that night, after Robert had gone to sleep, Chris said that he was sorry but that it had just been a knee-jerk reaction. He was not remorseful at all. I was horrified that he was so nonchalant about it, as if it was no big deal, because it was a big deal to me, a *really* big deal!

At first, when I looked back at that memory, I was intensely angry with myself for not deciding to leave Chris right after that happened. I wished that I had immediately called in an abuse report and filed for divorce the following day, but I did not have the perspective or clarity at the time. I had to learn to give myself grace because I did not understand the patterns of abuse that I understand now, and I had to forgive myself for the choices that I made when I was living in survival mode. I had to have empathy for the past version of myself, who was doing her very best to make sense of a highly confusing situation. I had to remind myself that I could not see the big picture then and that as a woman who was five months pregnant with a daughter on the way, my hope that Chris would change was greater than my fear that he would not.

Lesson: It is normal for victims of abuse to experience guilt for not having left earlier once they are out of the abuse dynamic and can see things clearly. Give yourself grace for not having been able to see the patterns when you were in the midst of them.

Additionally, when you are in an abuse dynamic, especially one that involves emotional abuse, it is highly confusing, and you begin to doubt yourself and lose trust in your own instincts. For example, Chris would repeatedly tell me that I overreacted to things and that I was too sensitive. After hearing this so many times, a part of me started believing it was the truth. Once out of the dynamic, I understood that he was deflecting (a covert abuse tactic)—making me feel guilty for having hurt feelings rather than taking responsibility for his actions that may have contributed to my feelings.

Lesson: It is valid to have and express hurt feelings in a relationship. It is not healthy for a partner to tell you that you are "too much" or "too sensitive" or to become angry with you when you express your feelings. A healthy partner will honor and respect your feelings.

As hard as it was for me to forgive Chris, by far the hardest person for me to forgive was myself. I would lie in bed night after night, unable to sleep, feeling a deep, gut-wrenching guilt for everything that I had done wrong as a mother. I deeply regretted the times that I had spanked Robert and the times I had lost my temper with him. I would replay painful scenes in my head, punishing myself with a tangible sort of suffering that I felt coursing through my entire body.

Then, of course, there was the enormous guilt for having chosen Chris as my children's father. I would obsessively think about all the unhealthy traits that he would teach my kids and all the times he would yell at them, making them feel guilty for insignificant things, making them feel scared, and looking at them with hatred the way that he had looked at me a thousand times. I would immerse myself in guilt and self-beat-up for not having left Chris the day after he back slapped Robert. Then, there was the guilt for not having spotted the red flags at the very beginning of my relationship with Chris. I could see it all so clearly now! How could I not have seen all of this before? How could I have been so blind, and why didn't I listen to my body when it told me so clearly again and again to run away from him?

Lesson: *Allow yourself to forgive yourself for everything you did while you were in survival mode. Know that you were doing your very best.*

Around that time, I watched a TED Talk on the importance of self-forgiveness and thought, *I have no idea how to access that.* The message made sense to me, but I had no clue how to even begin to forgive myself. It was a completely foreign concept to me at that time because I was so deeply immersed in my guilt and regret.

Years later, at a self-development retreat, I stood up and told my story in front of a group of women. The coach asked me if I had forgiven myself for what had happened, and I burst into tears. The truth is that I hadn't. I couldn't. I didn't know how to. There was a part of me that felt like I needed to hold on to the guilt and self-punishment to atone for what had happened and was still happening with Chris sharing custody of our kids. It took a few years, but the more inner work that I did and the more that I leaned into my spiritual practices, the more I released the guilt and shame and forgave myself. What I found was that the more I was able to forgive myself, the more I could allow love and joy to come back into my life.

Lesson: When you forgive yourself, it increases your ability to give love and to experience love. By letting go of your guilt and shame, you free up space in your energetic body to welcome in love and joy, which allows you to step into alignment with the highest version/expression of yourself.

So many of my memories, as well as what I continued to experience with Chris as a co-parent, made it very easy for me to hold on to my hatred toward him, and I did for many years. However, what I came to learn is that holding onto hatred was ultimately harmful to me and, by extension, to my kids. Choosing to cling to my hatred for Chris was only creating suffering for myself and blocking my capacity to expand and move forward in joy.

Lesson: Holding onto hatred toward another is ultimately harmful to yourself and will energetically block you from creating the life that you desire.

Through my self-development and spiritual work, I landed on a new belief that allows me to have compassion for everyone I encounter. My belief is this: Every person in every moment is doing the very best that they can based on what they have learned and the life experiences they have had. I was able to cultivate a deep love and even appreciation for Chris from this perspective, knowing that he was truly doing the best he could.

Lesson: *Every person in every moment is doing the very best that they can based on the life experiences that they have had up to that point. Knowing this allows us to practice forgiveness much more easily.*

Forgiveness does not mean that you condone unacceptable behaviors, and by forgiving, you are not choosing to continue to accept such behaviors. It doesn't mean that you don't have clear boundaries, and it doesn't mean that you don't walk away from toxic situations. You still walk away, and you continue to set healthy boundaries, but as you do this, you bless the person and send them love, knowing that they were doing the best that they could. When you cultivate this kind of forgiveness, you set yourself free.

In the simplest of terms, holding onto hatred feels bad. It feels bad to you, and it radiates out to everyone around you. Conversely, choosing to view those in your sphere through a lens of love feels good, and this, too, resonates to the people around you. It sounds so basic, and that is because it is, but that doesn't mean that it's always easy to practice. Many people think about forgiveness as something a person has to earn or deserve, but as many great spiritual teachers have taught, forgiveness is ultimately not for others—it is for you. It lifts the shackles off of your heart so that you can be free. Once I started leaning into forgiving Chris, I had more peace in my life, and I could accept my reality with him as my co-parent.

Lesson: *Forgiveness is not for the other person. It is for you. Forgiveness sets you free.*

It was important for me to study covert and emotional abuse so that I could understand what had happened and why I had allowed it to happen. It was important for me to understand so that I could name what I had experienced and be aware of it as I moved forward into other relationships. Once I had understood it, acknowledged it, and allowed myself to experience the emotions surrounding it without judgment, I was able to start letting it go. I began forgiving Chris for his behavior and forgiving myself for having accepted it. I was able to have compassion for the version of myself that had allowed herself to experience that kind of treatment, and I was able to have compassion for Chris's life experiences that had led to him acting the way that he did.

Until you let go of those heavy chains of hatred toward others as well as hatred toward yourself, you don't have enough space to truly love. Nor do you have the ability to be free enough to pursue the things in your life that you ultimately desire. For me personally, a radical paradigm shift allowed me to not only forgive Chris but also to have gratitude and love for him. A coach that I was working with invited me into a new outlook as I continued to struggle with co-parenting with Chris. Instead of seeing him as the villain in my life, I could choose to see him as a spiritual teacher. I could choose to be grateful for the lessons that he was making available for me to learn. One of these powerful lessons was learning how to stay in my own energy when I was with him and to set very strong boundaries of energetic and emotional protection.

Lesson: *When you can shift from seeing someone in your life as a villain and instead see them as a spiritual teacher, the negativity that you feel toward them is transformed into gratitude for the lessons that you are learning from them.*

Any person in your life that triggers or frustrates you can be seen as a teacher. Inevitably, if someone elicits a strong emotional reaction from you, that means that there is a lesson there for you. Ultimately, it is about you, not them. Though on the surface these people may frustrate the hell out of you, with a conscious shift of focus, you can inquire about what that person is revealing to you about you. They can be seen as beings who are here to help you step into the person that you're meant to be in this lifetime. Perhaps your souls even arranged these meetings for the purpose of creating the lessons that you were both meant to learn in this lifetime. When you can see a challenging person in your life from this perspective you can transform hatred and resentment into love and gratitude.

Lesson: When someone in your life stirs up strong emotional reactions in you, you can use it as an opportunity to look within yourself and ask what it is within you that has an opportunity to grow or strengthen from the situation at hand.

When I changed my perspective around Chris and began to appreciate him for what he was teaching me and to have compassion for the parts of him that continued to be challenging for me, my healing proc ess and path to personal liberation became much deeper. With this simple yet profound shift of perspective, I have become a stronger and more authentic person because I no longer allow my emotional state to be dependent on another person's behavior. When I momentarily forget and have a human freak-out moment, I bring myself back to my center and find my peace more quickly.

Lesson: You will never have control over someone else's behavior, but you always have control over how you choose to view, process, and respond to it. This is where your power (and your peace) comes from.

It helps me to remember that every person acts a certain way because of the experiences, programming, and paradigms that they have internalized for their entire life up to the moment that you are experiencing with him/her. All of these past experiences have formulated each person that we interact with. So, when you interact with someone who greatly triggers you, before going straight into reaction mode, take a breath and ponder where he/she may be coming from, as well as the lesson you may be able to learn from the interaction. You have no idea what they've been through that morning, that week, that month, that year. They could have lost a child. They could have lost their job. They could have grown up in intense poverty or with abusive parents. There's no way to know, but coming from the belief that everyone is truly doing their best, how can we make any other choice but to have compassion for everyone we meet?

CHAPTER FOUR LESSONS:

- It is normal for victims of abuse to experience guilt for not having left earlier once they are out of the abuse dynamic and can see things clearly. Give yourself grace for not having been able to see the patterns when you were in the midst of them.

- It is valid to have and express hurt feelings in a relationship. It is not healthy for a partner to tell you that you are "too much" or "too sensitive" or to become angry with you when you express your feelings. A healthy partner will honor and respect your feelings.

- Allow yourself to forgive yourself for everything you did while you were in survival mode. Know that you were doing your very best.

- When you forgive yourself, it increases your ability to give love and to experience love. By letting go of your guilt and shame, you free up space in your energetic body to welcome in love and joy, which allows you to step into alignment with the highest version/expression of yourself.

- Holding onto hatred toward another is ultimately harmful to yourself and will energetically block you from creating the life that you desire.

- Every person in every moment is doing the very best that they can based on the life experiences that they have had up to that point. Knowing this allows us to practice forgiveness much more easily.

- Forgiveness is not for the other person. It is for you. Forgiveness sets you free.

- When you can shift from seeing someone in your life as a villain and instead see them as a spiritual teacher, the negativity that you feel toward them is transformed into gratitude for the lessons that you are learning from them.

- When someone in your life stirs up strong emotional reactions in you, you can use it as an opportunity to look within yourself and ask what it is within you that has an opportunity to grow or strengthen from the situation at hand.

- You will never have control over someone else's behavior, but you always have control over how you choose to view, process, and respond to it. This is where your power (and your peace) comes from.

- When you forgive yourself, it increases your ability to be, do, and have what you want in life. Sometimes the only person in your way of moving forward is you.

CHAPTER 5
THE INNER WORK

"Today is a new day. Today is a day for you to begin creating a joyous, fulfilling life. Today is the day to begin to release all your limitations. Today is the day for you to learn the secrets of life. You can change your life for the better. You already have the tools within you to do so. These tools are your thoughts and your beliefs."
—Louise Hay

Before I attended the emotional intelligence training, I had not had much experience with personal development. I really had no idea the depth that the work could take when you really dove into it. The training that I attended made me realize how precious this life is and how we have such a finite time to walk on this planet in this lifetime. In the brief time that we are here, we can choose to wear masks and allow our life choices to be dictated by what we perceive others might think of us, or we can do the work to get in tune with who we really desire to be. Living from a space of conscious intention, we all have the potential to step into lives that we are passionate about and that we love.

So many people feel trapped in their lives. They wake up day in and day out in situations that they don't like, jobs they don't like, and with people they don't like. I know because I've been there. It's a horrible feeling to wake up with a feeling of dread in your gut about the day that lies before you. Until you get really clear about who you want to be in the world, what you want to create, and the life that you want to have, you're likely just walking through life on autopilot, making decisions based on past programming rather than making decisions that are truly in alignment with your highest self.

NOTE: The highest self here refers to the part of you that is eternal, the part that is never born and that never dies. Your highest self is God/Goddess/Source Energy within you.

Let's explore some of the different types of personal development work that will support you in living a life that lights you up.

Cultivating Awareness

Our thoughts create our emotions, and our emotions carry energetic vibrations. The frequency at which we vibrate will dictate the frequency of energy that we attract more of. So cultivating awareness of your thoughts and ultimately having dominion over them is essential in creating inner peace. It helps to start by acknowledging that just because you are thinking something doesn't mean it is true. It's just a thought, and thoughts that we repeat to ourselves again and again become beliefs.

As I mentioned earlier, depending on the families of origin that we are born into, we all formulate specific beliefs early on about who we are and what we are capable of. We create these beliefs on a subconscious level at a very young age before we're able to understand the world around us. All these beliefs will continue to inform us of who we believe we are and what we believe is possible for us.

For most people, these beliefs remain in the subconscious part of their brains, outside of their awareness and, therefore, outside of their capacity to change them. However, once you become aware of these beliefs, you gain the capacity to alter them and mold them into beliefs that support you in being and having what you desire in your life.

It is clear from research that even though we are aware of our consciousness, it is the unconscious mind operating quietly in the background that is really running our lives.
—N.S. Raghavan,
"We Are Mostly Driven by Our Subconscious Mind"[1]

An integral step toward creating a life that you desire is cultivating awareness around the subconscious beliefs that are working against you being, doing, and having what you want. By cultivating this awareness, you will be able to see where you have been confined by a limited paradigm. From there, you can consciously choose to expand your paradigm to include whatever you want to experience. In other words, once you identify the beliefs that are working against you, you can release them and replace them with beliefs that are working for you.

---

1. *NeuroInsights,* "We Are Mostly Driven by Our Subconscious Mind" last modified July 25, 2017, https://neuroinsights.in/2017/07/25/we-are-mostly-driven-by-our-subconscious-mind/.

Before I began my self-development journey, I never imagined that I would write a book or speak in front of large groups. It just wasn't something I saw as a possibility. This is because I held the subconscious belief that I was shy and my ideas weren't important or smart enough to share. Once I became aware of these beliefs, I was able to release them and replace them with the beliefs that I have ideas worthy of sharing and that I am energized and inspired by speaking on stage about subjects that I'm passionate about. Once my paradigm opened to these possibilities, I was able to consciously choose to pursue them.

Lesson: *You can change the limiting beliefs that you have about yourself by becoming aware of them. Once you are aware of them, you can consciously replace them with beliefs that support you in who you desire to be, what you desire to do, and the experiences you desire to have.*

The field of neuroscience has revealed that we are capable of rewiring the neural pathways in our brains. Neural pathways are nerve pathways in the brain that act as communication highways. Neuroplasticity is the ability of the brain to form new communication pathways in response to new learning or experience. We can actually change the shape of our brains by what we learn!

In other words, science has proven that we can replace a limiting belief that we've been carrying in our subconscious minds for years with new beliefs that support who we want to be by formulating new neural pathways. We can, quite literally, transform our lives simply by becoming aware of our beliefs and consciously choosing new ones that support and empower us. It takes mental awareness, and it takes repetition because the brain is building new pathways over old ones that are well-established, but if you stay committed to the work, the new belief will become your new truth, and you will let the old belief go.

Lesson: *The first step to replacing limiting beliefs is simply becoming aware of them. The second step is consciously deciding to release them every time you are aware of them popping up. Finally, you get to replace the old belief with a new belief that will support you!*

Daring to Dream

Most of us don't give ourselves permission to dream. We may have allowed ourselves to dream when we were children, but by the time we reach adulthood, most of those dreams have been replaced by life's obligations and responsibilities, as well as resentment, perhaps, for certain dreams that didn't come true. Many of us were told our dreams weren't possible or sensible, or maybe we were even told we were not capable of achieving them or that they were stupid. So, we left our dreams in the past with our child-selves and did what we felt that we had to do to survive.

However, studies show that when we are doing what we love, that is when we are the most productive and experience the most success. People who love the work that they do will always be better at their jobs than people who don't, and just imagine the state of the world if everyone loved what they did!

According to the *Forbes* article, "How To Get Into The 'Zone Of Genius' And Unlock Your Highest Potential," by Brianna Wiest, when you are operating within your zone of genius, "...[Y]ou capitalize on your natural abilities, which are innate, rather than learned. This is the state in which you get into 'flow,' find ceaseless inspiration, and seem to not only come up with work that is distinguished and unique but also do so in a way that excels far and beyond what anyone else is doing.[2]"

We are meant to do work that lights us up and inspires us. We are better at it and experience more joy, not only while working but in our lives in general. I used to believe work was supposed to be hard and strenuous, but like many beliefs that were not serving me, I consciously decided to replace this with the new belief that work should be fun, inspiring, and allow me copious amounts of free time for self-care and spending time with my family!

So this is your permission slip to ask yourself this magic question: "If I had a paintbrush and could paint myself the exact life that I desire (no holding back, no restrictions), what would it look like?" For just a few moments, allow yourself to dream without judging yourself or telling yourself it's not possible. Notice what dream comes up for you. Now, notice all the beliefs that come up to tell you that your dream is not possible—these are your limiting beliefs. Ask yourself what beliefs you would need to have in order to be able to pursue your dream—these are the new beliefs that you get to train yourself to believe (i.e. create new neural pathways in your brain).

Exercise: 1) *Choose a dream you would like to pursue,* 2) *Notice the thoughts that tell you your dream is impossible,* 3) *Ask yourself what beliefs you would need to have for your dream to be actualized,* 4) *Become aware of each time you have the disempowering thoughts and consciously replace them with empowering thoughts.*

---

2. Wiest, B. (2024, February 20). *How to get into the "Zone of Genius" and unlock your highest potential.* Forbes. https://www.forbes.com/sites/briannawiest/2018/09/26/how-to-get-into-the-zone-of-genius-and-unlock-your-highest-potential/

A belief is no more than a thought that we think over and over again and accept as truth. To train yourself to believe something new, you have to consciously release your old (limiting) belief and seek out all possible evidence to support that your new belief is true. A function of the brain, your reticular activating system, will actually help you do this. The reticular activating system (RAS) is the part of the brain that filters the information that you take in. We have so much information coming at us all the time, and we cannot process it all. The RAS filters out the information that it deems to be irrelevant and allows what it perceives to be important to get through to us.

So the more we put our attention on something, the more we will notice that thing, and the more we seek out evidence that a certain belief is true, the more we will see evidence to support this belief. For example, if I want to create a successful acting career for myself, it would be beneficial for me to read success stories of small-town people who achieved acting success rather than seeking out stories of failed actors. What you put your attention on is what you will see more of.

Lesson: You get to expand your paradigm from where you are currently to where you desire to be in the future, and you start this expansion by choosing to believe that it is possible.

Manifestation

One concept that I knew nothing about before I started my exploration into the self-development world was the concept of manifestation. Manifestation is the way that we consciously (or unconsciously) attract people, things, and experiences into our lives. This is because what you think about and what you put your attention on is what you will create more of in your life. We are all powerful creators of our own realities. On one level, we create our own realities because everything that we experience is filtered through our minds. We create interpretations that color our experiences. We can create disempowering interpretations or empowering ones. Once we become aware of our thoughts, we can choose to create interpretations that make us feel good and that allow us to experience peace.

Let's say you decide that you want to change jobs because you don't like your boss. If you go to work every day putting your focus on how much you hate your boss and continually complain about your boss, then you are likely to continue experiencing a boss you dislike and keep yourself stuck in that job or one that is similar.

Conversely, if you go to that same job, but instead of focusing on the boss that you don't like, you find positive things to focus on, such as the awesome money that you're earning, or your hilarious coworker who makes you laugh, then you are already shifting your own personal experience into a much more positive one while you are simultaneously leaving space for the Universe to create a new employment possibility for you that is in alignment with what you desire.

Getting attached to manifesting particular things is where people get tripped up. There are a lot of people out there who claim that they can help you manifest concrete things into your life quickly and easily. For me personally, it didn't happen this way. When I first started experimenting with the concept of manifestation, after a while, I became overwhelmed and frustrated. What I learned was that manifestation with attachment to a particular outcome didn't work for me. On the other hand, manifestation accompanied by true surrender and trust in the Universe *did* work.

I'll give you an example of this. For a long time, I really wanted my kids to go to a certain private school. I had seen it online, and I loved so many things about it. It offered the children so much freedom, and it honored each individual child. I got really set on this idea that my kids had to go to this school, which was in a different city. I worked really hard with all the tools that I had to manifest this reality. I meditated often, thinking about how I would feel when my children went there. I did visualization exercises of my kids being at the school, etc. Meanwhile, my deeper belief was that moving to a new city was not possible because I did not have the legal right to move unless Chris was on board, which he wasn't. So even while I was sitting in meditation and doing all the visualization practices to bring this school into our reality, my rational brain was saying, *This is really not possible.*

I went through the frustration of wondering what I was doing wrong. Why was this not working? What was wrong with me? After sitting in this place for quite some time, I started studying about surrender. I learned more and more to lean into the practice of letting go and having full trust that God/Goddess/Spirit is creating everything for me and my kids in the perfect way, in divine timing.

When you trust that the Universe has got your back, the fear and anxiety go away as well as the attachment to specific outcomes. When I let go of the attachment to my kids going to that particular school, and I started seeing all the positives of their current public school, a new private school popped up in our community. On top of that, I was able to get a scholarship for my kids, which got Chris on board with the kids going there as well.

The lesson I took from this was that when I gave up the attachment to the exact thing I wanted (the private school) and I developed gratitude and full acceptance for what was currently present (the public school), I made space for the Universe to do its work and create the perfect school for my kids at the perfect time. Had I stayed attached to the first school as the only possibility and generated negative emotions about the public school where they were, I would not have created the space for the perfect school opportunity to be delivered, and I would have continued to experience the negative things about the public school that I was putting my focus on. The most important part of this process is trusting that the Universe always has your highest and best interest at heart, even if you can't see it or figure it out from where you stand.

Lesson: *Manifestation will only work for you when you remain unattached to specific outcomes and fully accept and have gratitude for your present situation as you remain open to what the Universe may bring. You must trust that God/Goddess/Spirit is delivering you the perfect things in perfect timing and surrender to this inner knowing.*

Visualization

I adore the powerful practice of visualization. Visualization is a practice in which you imagine the things in your mind that you would like to experience in reality. Truthfully, it is something that we are all doing all the time. We are just not conscious that we are doing it. Often, we visualize worst-case scenarios and outcomes without being aware of it, which ultimately makes us feel bad and lowers our vibration. Consciously practicing visualization allows you to actually take control of what you envision for yourself, and it's really fun!

You get to create and tweak your own personal visualization practice, but I'll just tell you what works for me. My practice consists of sitting in silence or with instrumental music. I often use the Tibetan singing bowl sound from the White Noise app or 528 Hz music. I simply start by getting quiet and asking myself, *What feels good?* Then I allow myself to daydream about anything that makes me feel happy. If I start getting distracted, then I ask myself the question again: *What feels good?* I allow my imagination to go wherever it wants to go as long as it feels good. I may skip from image to image, for example, from dancing with my kids to climbing a mountain with a group of friends to kissing a new lover in a fabulous setting. I don't judge what comes up; I just enjoy the feeling of it.

Often, I have gotten stuck in the details. For example, let's say I'm visualizing an awesome date with a guy who inspires me. I may visualize meeting him at a restaurant and then find myself debating over whether another restaurant would be better or if I want him to pick me up at my house or not. When I find myself asking these questions that are taking me out of my feeling body and into my mental body, I simply ask myself the question again: *What feels good?* In the visualization, you don't want to get lost in the details or whether your rational brain thinks your visualization is possible or not, but rather to connect to whatever imagery makes you *feel* good.

The important thing in the visualization process is being in the *emotion* that you want to experience. It is not the time to try to figure out how to make a specific thing happen. You don't have to worry about that. Just see the images and feel the feelings. Simple!

Lesson: Visualization is about feeling the emotion that you want to feel. Don't let your mental brain take over with all of its questions and doubts. Just allow yourself to move from image to image of what feels good for you and lean into the feeling.

Meditation

The most powerful practice, hands down, that I have found for staying connected with your higher self and experiencing peace is the practice of meditation. I meditate almost every day. The days that I'm not able to meditate, usually because of my children, I notice a tangible difference in my connection to myself, in my connection to the Divine, and in my connection to my inner peace.

I think a lot of people get overwhelmed by the idea of meditation. I have heard many people express that they aren't good at meditation, that it feels too hard, or that they can't turn off their thoughts. Perhaps some teachers have made meditation sound too complicated. In truth, it's very simple.

Meditation is simply sitting in silence and watching your thoughts. It doesn't mean that you have to stop your thoughts. It just means that you're aware of your thoughts as they go by, and you don't judge them. The more you practice this, the more your thoughts will slow down, and the more peaceful you will feel. The key is cultivating awareness of what is going on within yourself. You will become aware of the thoughts constantly running through your mind, and you will get to know your inner self much more intimately. Also, when you create the space for yourself to sit in silence, you're opening up to the inspiration of the universe, and you're cultivating your connection with the Divine that is always accessible from within.

Letting go of Judgment, Shame, and Guilt

Another critical practice that I have found on my path toward peace is letting go of judgment—judgment of self as well as judgment of others. Often, a judgment that you have against another person is truly a judgment that you have against yourself on some level. Additionally, the self-judgmental thoughts that you have about yourself often did not even come from you. They may have come from a parent, teacher, or other influential figure in your life. That person judged you in some way, and you internalized that judgment of yourself, usually without being conscious of it. When you can simply love yourself and others with all of your/their perceived faults, when you can accept everyone and everything as it is, that is when you will feel peace.

Equally as important along the journey to self-acceptance is the releasing of shame and guilt. We all carry shame and guilt for certain things that we did in our past. Shame and guilt carry very low vibrations and take up a lot of energetic space. The best thing we can do when we become aware of the guilt and shame that we are clinging to is to consciously choose to let it go. That may sound overly simple, and that is because it is. It is a choice.

Let's say you are holding on to guilt because of something specific you did in your past, and you just can't seem to let yourself off the hook for it. A very simple practice you can employ when you become aware of the guilt is to say, "I surrender this to the Universe. I choose to let it go." At first it will still feel like it is there. Your mind will tell you that it can't be that easy and that this simple proclamation couldn't possibly work. Allow yourself to simply stay open to the possibility that it *could* work, and continue the process each time the guilt presents itself. You will begin to see over time that the guilt begins to fade. Trust that the Universe is alchemizing it for you.

Not only does it not serve you to hold on to these emotions, but it weighs you down energetically and holds you back from embodying the highest version of yourself. If you desire additional support around learning how to let go of thoughts, emotions, and feelings that don't serve you, I recommend reading *The Sedona Method* by Hale Dwoskin or *Letting Go: The Pathway of Surrender* by David R. Hawkins.

Emotions are not meant to be pushed down or spiritually bypassed, but once they are acknowledged and accepted, they are meant to be released. The most powerful way to release emotions is to simply allow yourself to feel them—to be present with them without judging them. After I allow myself to experience an emotion, I surrender it to the Universe. We cannot travel back in time and change what we did or what we experienced, so hanging onto those emotions is simply taking up real estate in your energetic body that is weighing you down.

Lesson: *When you surrender an emotion to your higher power, you are freed from it, and you will experience a lightness that accompanies acceptance of what is.*

So many of us in the early periods of our lives were taught to hold emotions in, or we were shamed for having big emotions. To keep ourselves safe or to keep ourselves from experiencing punishment or external shame, we learned to shut our emotions down and swallow them. As adults, most of us are walking around with an abundance of repressed and unresolved emotions. When we consistently hold on to low vibrational emotions and don't allow ourselves to acknowledge or release them, they can end up expressing as disease in our bodies. Looking at them and then letting them go will set us free.

Somatic Work

An element of self-development work that I have found to be an integral part of the healing process for me and my clients is somatic work. Somatic means relating to the body, especially as it is distinct from the mind. Many therapeutic modalities place a large emphasis on talking through things, but research shows that trauma and subconscious patterning get stuck in our feeling bodies. You can talk for hours, days, and even years about something, but in order to be truly free of it, you must release the energy from your body.

There is definitely some work that can be done in the mental realm, but I've learned that the deeper levels of healing come from accessing the sensations of the body itself. With the guidance of a trauma-informed coach or therapist, you can be safely guided through the process of feeling your emotions and letting them leave your body in a safe and supported space. This can pertain to difficult emotions that you are aware of, as well as emotions that have been suppressed in your subconscious. The coach holds a space for you to let those emotions out in a safe way and in an environment that is completely loving and non-judgmental. It is intense work but absolutely worth it for the space and freedom it creates.

If you don't have the capacity in your present situation to hire a coach, here are a few ways to encourage emotional release on your own:

1. Turn on music that carries the energy of the emotion that feels present for you, and dance your heart out! Close your eyes and feel. It doesn't matter how you're moving your body. It only matters how it makes you feel. (If you are desiring an anger release, make sure you are in a place that feels safe and in which you can be as loud as you want. Turn on angry music, and let yourself rage. Say whatever you want! Yell, scream, kick, punch. Tell everyone and everything you are mad at to fuck off! Allow the emotion to flow from you without judgment.) If you are feeling sad, turn on sad music and let yourself cry your eyes out. Once you feel complete, choose to let it go and surrender it to the Universe.

2. If there is something you want to express to someone but aren't able to or don't feel safe to, write them a letter saying anything and everything you want to say and then burn it (let it go).

3. Free-journal by allowing yourself to write swiftly and freely without judging or editing yourself. Just allow it to flow! (I also like to draw pictures when I do this.)

*When you finish your emotional release, choose to let it go and move on with your day with a new lightness of spirit. You have cleared space that you can now fill with joy and gratitude.

Cultivating Your Intuition

Along with the somatic work, you can also do your own inner work of cultivating a deeper relationship with your intuition. In our society, we are taught to navigate our lives from the mind, from the intellect, but I believe that our true power lies in following our intuition. As we bring more and more awareness to how our body is feeling from moment to moment and allow this to be our guide, we will cultivate a deeper relationship with the truest part of ourselves. The more we live from that place, the more we will be in alignment with our highest purpose, and the more we will live the lives that we're truly meant to live.

As I mentioned before, meditation is a huge part of cultivating inner awareness, but also in a very simple way, simply checking in with how your body is feeling at different points throughout your day will bring you into a more intimate relationship with your intuition and where it is directing you.

Our truth comes from our highest self, the part of us that is tapped into Universal Intelligence. When we're tapped into our intuition and our bodies, we're allowing the Divine to lead us. Outside of meditation, which has been the most potent way for me to get in touch with my inner self, some other ways that I have found to cultivate this relationship are spending time in nature, doing breathwork, making/listening to uplifting music, allowing yourself to be creative in your favorite way, and dancing!

It also helps me to close my eyes at different moments throughout my day to check in with how I'm feeling. Even just taking one minute or less will give you insight into your internal world that is so easily muted by all the noise that most of us encounter in our day-to-day lives. So much of what we navigate each day invites our attention to move outward. Social media, advertisements, TV, and the news all pull our focus outside of ourselves and into the realm of comparison and judgment. When we take time to be away from these outside influences and bring our focus inward, we are creating the space for ourselves to be guided by our strongest and most trustworthy source—our own inner knowing.

CHAPTER FIVE LESSONS:

- You can change the limiting beliefs that you have about yourself by becoming aware of them. Once you are aware of them, you can consciously replace them with beliefs that support you in who you desire to be, what you desire to do, and the experiences you desire to have.

- The first step to replacing limiting beliefs is simply becoming aware of them. The second step is consciously deciding to release them every time you are aware of them popping up. Finally, you get to replace the old belief with a new belief that will support you!

- You get to expand your paradigm from where you are currently to where you desire to be in the future, and you start this expansion by choosing to believe that it is possible.

- Manifestation will only work for you when you remain unattached to specific outcomes and fully accept and have gratitude for your present situation as you remain open to what the Universe may bring. You must trust that God/Goddess/Spirit is delivering you the perfect things in perfect timing and surrender to this inner knowing.

- Visualization is about feeling the emotion that you want to feel. Don't let your mental brain take over with all of its questions and doubts. Just allow yourself to move from image to image of what feels good for you and lean into the feeling.

- When you surrender an emotion to your higher power, you are freed from it, and you will experience a lightness that accompanies acceptance of what is.

ACCEPTANCE AND SURRENDER

"When we are finally and fully surrendered on all components,
the answer will be there waiting for us."
—David R. Hawkins,
Letting Go: The Pathway of Surrender

One of the scariest times of my entire life was when my son said some things that made me and his play therapist believe there may be some sexual abuse occurring at his dad's house. This event occurred before I had found my spiritual footing, and I was reacting in full fear mode. I was frightened beyond measure, and I decided to file an injunction (a hearing in front of a judge to try to acquire immediate custody and protection from the child's other parent).

The night before the injunction, I was extremely anxious as my attorney was unavailable (long story), and I could not find another attorney willing to help me on such short notice. I have never experienced this level of anxiety before or since. In the darkness of my house after both of my kids were asleep, I went into the kitchen and compiled all the information I would present to the judge, knowing fully that I wasn't a lawyer and that I had no clue what I was doing. I felt my children's safety and well-being depended on me showing up and defending them. I don't think I slept at all that night.

The following morning, my mom went with me to the hearing, but she was not permitted to go into the courtroom with me. I walked alone up to the small table to the left of Chris and his attorney and sat by myself with my notebook full of scribbled notes. When it was my turn to speak, the judge asked me a few specific questions but would not listen to anything further I had to say. He listened to the testimony of the representative from the Department of Children and Families (a twenty-something in her first year on the job) who had interviewed both me and Chris and who had concluded that there was no evidence to prove that there was abuse going on at Chris's. The judge told me that I had to continue taking the kids to their dad's on his appointed nights and that if I didn't, I would be in contempt of the court. That was the end of it.

I stood up from that table and dragged myself out of the room. I felt that I was in a horrible dream. When I exited the room, my mom was there waiting for me, and I fell into her arms and wept. She walked me into the elevator and held me as I continued to cry. This is when I knew that there was nothing that could be done.

As a mother, there is nothing worse than feeling like you can't protect your children. I felt so angry at God. I remember driving one day and yelling in a fit of rage at the top of my lungs, "God, why would you give me children and not let me protect them?!"

I couldn't understand it. I couldn't make sense of it. Why would I be given children I couldn't take care of? What was the purpose of that? It seemed so cruel. For many years after that, I was basically obsessed with wanting full custody of my children.

I believed that they were experiencing so much harm from their dad and that they were going to be irrevocably emotionally harmed. I believed that my son would likely take on the attitudes and behaviors of his father, thus making him unable to have healthy relationships in the future and very likely making him an abusive future husband and father. I believed that my daughter would learn that it was okay to experience abuse and that she would likely be the victim of abuse in her future relationships.

Robert and Elizabeth would often cry and not want to go to Chris's. One heartbreaking night after Robert's seventh birthday party, we went back to Chris's apartment to open Robert's presents. It was technically Chris's night, but since it was his birthday, Robert had asked me to ask Chris if he could sleep at my house. Chris immediately became red in the face and started yelling at the two of us for even proposing the idea. This made Robert begin to sob immediately. Elizabeth was silent and stunned. I knew from experience that if I were to have stayed, it would only have accelerated Chris's anger, so I willed myself to leave. I saw Elizabeth blankly staring at me as the door closed and heard Chris continuing to yell at Robert as he blubbered out, "I'm sorry, Daddy. I'm sorry, Daddy," over and over again through his sobs. It was utterly heartbreaking, and to this day it remains a traumatic event for me and my kids.

There were more experiences like this than I can count when I was a witness to my children's suffering, and I was powerless to change it. At the time, I resisted it fully. It made me sick to my stomach. It made me want to rage and punch walls, and it made me hate Chris.

Another time, when I was at Chris's apartment dropping the kids off, Robert began to cry and wouldn't calm down. I asked Chris if he would turn on a TV show so that Robert could calm down before I left. I didn't want to leave him in that state, but Chris refused and said Robert would be fine. I decided not to leave Robert when he was inconsolable because I felt like I was abandoning him. So I said I would stay until he calmed down.

This greatly angered Chris, and when he saw that I was serious, he began to yell at me to get out. He started calling me an *intruder* and telling me that this was my fault for wanting a divorce in the first place. I remember standing there, my entire body trembling in front of this large man in a rage, but I stood my ground. This made Chris continue to escalate to the point where his yelling was unbearable until, finally, I ended up calling 911. Situations like this showed me that resisting the situation at hand with Chris only made it bigger and downright explosive.

Over the years of navigating the legal system around the custody of my children, I felt a lot of hopelessness and experienced profound suffering. I kept returning to the belief that if I could only get full custody, then my children and I could finally have peace, but I felt stuck after speaking with a number of lawyers who all said that there was nothing I could do until there was hard proof of abuse. Additionally, at least in the area where I live, emotional and verbal abuse are not enough to constitute *abuse* to the *system*. I had also learned that reporting abuse to the Department of Children and Families only ever resulted in inconclusive investigations and a rising suspicion that I was placing ideas in my children's heads. Unless someone witnessed his abusive behavior firsthand, there was nothing that I could do, and he was and continues to be very intentional about keeping such behavior behind closed doors.

So I was left with a choice to either cultivate radical acceptance of my reality or to continue to fight it. As Carl Jung says, "What you resist persists." By beating myself up about it and continually trying to fight it, I was essentially living in hell on earth. I was sad, frustrated, anxious, nervous, angry, and bitter, and I was not able to move forward in a positive way with my life.

As the comfort of my spiritual beliefs grew, I began to oscillate between striving for full custody and surrendering to what was. I wondered if surrendering was just giving up. *Was it selling out on my children? Was I acting out of fear?* I went back and forth for years. *Should I hire another lawyer? Was there anything else I could do? If I surrendered, was that just me not fighting hard enough for my kids? Was I being weak, not wanting to go back into another fight with Chris?* After all, if I didn't advocate for my children, who would? Ultimately, though, I surrendered—I let it go. I had to because it was eating me up from the inside out.

The moment I stepped into real acceptance, I began to cultivate my own inner peace. Surrender didn't mean that if or when there would be an opportunity to take action, I wouldn't. It simply meant that as long as it was clear that there was nothing I could do, resisting my reality was only creating suffering. If I wanted to experience any level of peace in my life, I had to let it go.

Lesson: *The moment you accept your reality, you will be able to access inner peace.*

Once I truly surrendered to my custody situation and accepted that this was my children's journey to take with their dad, I began to feel a huge weight lift from me energetically. I knew in my heart that I had advocated for them to the best of my ability.

By being in continual resistance to what was, I had been creating suffering, not only for myself but for everyone involved, including my kids. My inner resistance created ongoing turmoil that affected my thoughts, emotions, energy, and health. It trickled down into how I mothered my children because it made me angry, irritable, sad, and depressed. When Robert would have emotional meltdowns, I would project my anger onto him because I felt that his breakdowns were a direct result of how his dad was treating him, which pissed me off! It made me feel powerless and scared of the future as I would project negative visualizations of future possibilities onto my children.

Through my experience, I ultimately learned that surrender isn't weak. Surrender isn't giving up. Surrender is simply accepting what is so that you can be at peace, step back, and let Divine Consciousness work on your behalf. I cultivated the belief that everything is happening for me, unfolding perfectly in divine timing. I learned that you can let go of the illusion of control when you release your tight grip on specific outcomes and lean into your faith in the Universe. Not only do you feel more at peace, but by releasing your obsession with control, you create space for the Universe to do its thing (which will always be greater than anything your mind can create on its own).

Lesson: When you allow yourself to surrender to what is, you are creating space for the Universe to work things out in ways that you could not have facilitated on your own.

Surrendering also enabled me to let go of regret. I knew that in every moment, I had done the best I could in accordance with my current ability.

Lesson: When you adopt the belief that everything is happening for you, then you can no longer be a victim. You can trust the process, and you can trust the divine timing of your life. You are able to see that everything in your life is working for your highest good and for the highest good of all.

In *The Greatest Secret*, Rhonda Byrne teaches that consciousness/awareness says *yes* to everything. When you say *no*, you are in resistance to your situation, and that immediately creates suffering. Conversely, when you say *yes* to what is happening, you create peace instantaneously. Once you become aware of your thoughts, you always have the choice to either accept or to be in resistance to what unfolds before you.

To give a basic illustration of this, imagine you're driving, and you come upon a traffic jam. At that moment, you have a choice. You can either get angry and let it ruin your day, or you can accept the reality and choose to embrace it by taking the extra time to call a friend or listen to a few great songs. The first choice creates suffering, and the second choice creates peace and maybe even joy!

Lesson: *When you say yes to what is in front of you, you allow yourself to stay in the flow and, therefore, open to intuitive hits that may instruct you on your next move. However, when you say no, you are in immediate resistance and therefore cut yourself off from your connection to God/Goddess/Source and from your intuition.*

Divine consciousness says *yes* to everything. This kind of acceptance allows for flow. It allows for the Universe to take care of circumstances for you. Surrendering to my reality with my kids made all of our lives better. When I was living in resistance, my kids could feel my fear, worry, and anger, but once I was able to let it go, they could feel my peace and acceptance. Because children co-regulate their nervous systems with their parents, once my nervous system was regulated (at peace) it allowed my kids to tap into their inner peace rather than picking up on and taking on my fear and anger.

Surrendering is not weak. It actually takes a lot of courage and can feel quite scary at first because we are so used to fighting for control. Surrendering requires that you set your ego aside and allow what *is* to simply *be*. It doesn't mean that you don't take aligned action when it feels right, but when you do take action, it isn't from a place of strain, struggle, or fighting. It's from a place of flow, and it feels easy. When you surrender to the divine order of things, you are creating a space for the infinite field of possibilities to dazzle you with what is truly possible. It can create much bigger, grander things for you than you can even imagine from your limited human vantage point.

Surrendering is also one of the most effective ways to manifest favorable things in your life. Manifesting doesn't come from pushing and striving. It can't come from force. It can only come from the gentle energy of surrender and trust. When you know you really want something and you become attached to a specific way that that thing needs to come into your life, then you're creating limitations that may block that thing from coming at all.

For so long, I told myself that my kids and I could only be happy if I had full custody, but what I really wanted on a deeper, more profound level was peace, love, joy, and the best outcome for myself and my children. So I chose to trust that the Universe had a bigger plan for us, even if I couldn't see the full path from my limited perspective.

By clinging and being attached to having full custody, I wasn't allowing myself to be open to the myriad of other possibilities that existed. Letting go of the fight and surrendering to my reality allowed me to be open to the plethora of possibilities that the Universe had available for all of us that would result in the highest and best outcomes. When you let Spirit work through you and you release your attachment to things happening in a certain way at a certain time, then you create the space for Spirit to paint a much bigger, bolder picture for you. Surrendering to what is in my life has afforded me a deep peace that has made me a better mother, a better friend, and a more loving and giving human on this planet.

Everything is happening for you, and everything is unfolding perfectly in divine timing, so you might as well surrender to what is in front of you and trust that your higher power is taking care of everything for you.

CHAPTER SIX LESSONS:

- The moment you accept your reality, you will be able to access inner peace

- When you allow yourself to surrender to what is, you are creating space for the Universe to work things out in ways that you could not have facilitated on your own.

- When you adopt the belief that everything is happening for you, then you can no longer be a victim. You can trust the process, and you can trust the divine timing of your life. You are able to see that everything in your life is working for your highest good and for the highest good of all.

- When you say yes to what is in front of you, you allow yourself to stay in the flow and, therefore, open to intuitive hits that may instruct you on your next move. However, when you say no, you are in immediate resistance and therefore cut yourself off from your connection to God/Goddess/Source and from your intuition.

- Everything is happening for you, and everything is unfolding perfectly in divine timing, so you might as well surrender to what is in front of you and trust that your higher power is taking care of everything for you.

CHAPTER 7
A SPIRITUAL PATH

"When marriages end or we lose loved ones, or things seem to fall apart in our lives, we may suffer a lot, but very often it's through our suffering that we begin to wonder what life is all about. Many of the Enlightened Sages have gone through immense suffering, and it was their suffering that led them to question life intensely, and which ultimately led them to the truth of who they are."
—Rhonda Byrne,
The Greatest Secret

When I left my marriage, I found myself in a place of complete existential dilemma. It was a really scary place to be. I felt like my footing had been pulled completely out from underneath me. Prior to pursuing divorce, I had found comfort in Christianity, and I was able to access a certain amount of peace from the belief that there was a father who was taking care of me. I found peace in the ability to ask for forgiveness and in the trust that I would be forgiven. I felt supported by the idea that I could pray for something, that God was listening to my prayers, and that miracles could happen.

However, my divorce process and the experience of navigating it with my church had changed me. I felt deeply disappointed that I had confided in my pastor about the first time my ex had slapped Robert in the face, and he hadn't advised me to leave the marriage or to report the abuse.

I felt equally saddened that an older mentor in the church, with whom I had vulnerably shared my journey, also didn't point out to me that I was in a cycle of abuse. Perhaps the reason my mentor and pastor weren't able to support me was simply that they themselves were not educated about abuse. Nevertheless, I felt saddened that the people I had confided in hadn't advocated for me and my children or empowered me to flee from the abuse we were experiencing.

Additionally, in the months leading up to deciding to leave my marriage, I had reached out to two biblical counselors who were highly recommended by people at my church. Soon after Chris put his hand on my throat, I came to the realization that my counselor's goal was not to protect me and my children, but to keep our marriage intact.

It was downright shocking to me that—after I was pushed up against the wall with my husband's hand on my throat—there would be anyone who would encourage me to stay in the marriage! I was utterly flabbergasted and couldn't wrap my head around it. My pastors were clear that they believed me, and they kindly listened to me as I shared my story, but their bottom line was fighting for the marriage, not keeping me and my kids safe.

It became clear that to have the strength and resolve to move toward divorce, I would have to break away from my relationship with the church and with the biblical counselors. They were all fighting for the marriage, and I was fighting for a safe and peaceful existence for myself and my children. I was listening to my intuition, and I was taking action that expressed that abuse is not okay and that staying married is not more important than walking away from destructive and unacceptable behavior.

Lesson: For any woman who is in a relationship that is abusive or toxic, you must listen to your own inner voice and not to anyone else around you. If you know in your heart that you need to leave, then that is what you must do, no matter what anyone else says, even if they are in a position of leadership over you.

My experience with the Christian leaders in my life had created a large crack in my faith in the Christian church. It opened up some deep spiritual questioning, and though it was really uncomfortable not to know what I believed, I now see it as a blessing because it opened me up to be available to a paradigm shift that led me to where I am today. It liberated me to be able to open up to all the spiritual concepts that have since revolutionized my life.

I also realized as I looked back over the pattern of my life that both of my husbands had greatly influenced my religious views at different phases of my life. I had adopted both Francis's and Chris's beliefs when I got into relationships with them, and I knew that it was time for me to figure out what I believed, independent of everyone and everything around me. It was time to go within and figure out what my own personal truth was.

Of course, this is quite a scary place to be, especially when you're used to defining your world in a certain way. When you make sense of everything around you from the perspective of one religion, and then you start sensing cracks in it and things about it that don't make sense to you, it's extremely destabilizing and scary.

It was also very challenging for me to step away from my church's support system. I struggled with this for quite some time, as I live in a small, conservative town with a very limited spiritual community outside of the Christian church. I found myself feeling very isolated. Looking back, I see that this was the perfect place for me to dive into my own spiritual investigation, and so it began.

My prayer every night would simply be, "Please show me the truth. Please show me the truth," not even knowing who I was praying to. At first, I was afraid to share my new beliefs out of fear of being challenged or rejected. Still, I allowed myself to move forward on my journey of exploration. I realized that it was a slow and gentle unfolding of a new truth that made sense to my heart, soul, and mind. It was between me and the Divine and no one else.

I started listening to new podcasts and audiobooks. I dove into reading authors like Eckhart Tolle, Rhonda Byrne, and others. I let go of the fear of what other people thought about my beliefs. I even let go of the fear that if I was wrong, the Christian God I had believed in for so long would punish me for eternity. What I ultimately found is a greater level of peace than I've ever experienced before, even with all the suffering that I experienced along the way.

In *The Greatest Secret*, Rhonda Byrne explains that the only purpose in life is to be the totality of who we are. So who are we? We are each unique expressions of divine consciousness—unique expressions of God/Goddess. On a spiritual plane of existence, we are consciousness/awareness that is effortless, loving, and completely without fear. In contrast, on the earthly plane, we have the human experience of being separate body-minds with individual perception.

Rhonda explains that the more we tap into this consciousness/awareness, the more we can live in freedom, peace, and bliss—all of which come from the inside out. Tapping into this awareness can be done as easily as asking yourself, *Am I aware?* and then paying attention to that part of yourself that is aware of your thoughts. It is the part of you that is able to observe your own thinking, as if from afar. By asking this question, *Am I aware?* and paying attention, you can identify that there is a conscious presence within you that is able to observe your thoughts. It is a part of you that is aware, outside of your thinking mind.

Lesson: *You are not your thoughts. You are not your mind. You are not your body. You are divine consciousness having a human experience.*

This consciousness/awareness is the part of you that is connected to every other being on the planet because, ultimately, we are all individual and unique expressions of the one great loving energy that many people call God. When you are tapped into this grander part of you, you are aware that you are always and forever connected to all other beings. You are aware that you have direct access to Universal Intelligence because that is what you are made of. We are all, at our source, the same energy. We are made from the only energy that will endure throughout time, and that is the energy of love. From this vantage point, there is no other option but to love everyone we encounter because, on a macro level, they are you, and you are them. We are all one.

When you live from this place of consciousness/awareness, you're able to observe the thoughts that are constantly moving through your mind. Your thoughts don't stop, but you don't have to engage with them, and you certainly don't have to believe them. They are constantly moving, but many (if not most) of your thoughts are not supportive or even true. Your thoughts, your body, your mind, and your human identity are not who you are. When you die, your thoughts and your human form will be no longer but your soul—your consciousness/awareness—is never born and will never die. This part of you can never be harmed. If you carry this knowledge with you, you will no longer fear death because you know that whatever happens to your physical form, your soul will remain untarnished.

Lesson: *Your soul—your consciousness/awareness—is never born and will never die.*

In every moment, you have the choice of where you put your focus. You can focus on the perceived problems of your life, or you can focus on the fact that whatever happens in this lifetime, you and those you love will always be together because, ultimately, you are a part of the same field of energy that you never left. You can choose to zoom in and focus on all the details of your human stresses, or you can choose to zoom out and connect with the greater awareness that is our truest essence. When you are able to zoom out, you access peace because you know that all is ultimately well.

From the perspective of interconnectedness, it becomes easier to cultivate a deep love for everyone and everything in your world. When you move from this place of love, not only do you feel more peace, but things just start happening more easily in your life. You get in the flow because you are moving from a place of inspiration rather than from pushing and being driven by the mind. You naturally raise your energetic vibration, and your thoughts and emotions are naturally more positive. As a result of your higher energetic vibration, you attract more favorable things into your life. You make the world a better place by cultivating this peace within yourself because you radiate the energy to everyone and everything around you.

When I observe my mind, I see my thoughts as they go by. I notice my thoughts, but *I* am not my thoughts. When you connect to your awareness, you connect to your truest nature. You connect to the part of you that is eternal. From this place, you can access peace, joy, and absolute acceptance of what is. There is no more fear of the opinions of others. You're able to disconnect from your ego, from all the striving and trying and wanting to be more and do more and have more. You are able to let go of that never-ending ladder to a better career, more money, or whatever it is that you tell yourself you have to be, do, or have in order to be okay. You realize that there is nothing you have to do in order to be good enough because you are already divine perfection, and so is everyone else.

From this place of knowing, you can access the truest form of self-love and the truest form of love for others. When you see others as being eternally connected to you, as the beingness that we all are, then you can ultimately only love others, no matter how they're showing up in your life. As I have stretched more and more into this worldview, I have found that it's infinitely easier to be my authentic self because it really doesn't matter what anyone else thinks of me. I'm here to be the fullest expression of my unique body and mind in this lifetime. Nothing and no one can touch that.

Lesson: *Nothing and no one's opinion or interpretation of you has any bearing on who you actually are.*

My new spiritual outlook was what ultimately empowered me to find peace with Chris and with my kids spending time with him. I believe we choose our parents before we come into these lives. We choose them, and they choose us because we all have certain spiritual lessons that we are meant to learn and certain things we are meant to co-create and accomplish with everyone we come across in this lifetime. From this perspective, I was able to cultivate peace around the relationship between my kids and their dad because I knew they had something to learn from him that would serve their souls' growth in this lifetime.

Lesson: It is up to you to create interpretations of your life that feel good to think about. By creating positive interpretations, you are raising your energetic vibration, which will attract more of that higher vibration energy into your life.

I realized that it was up to me to create interpretations of my life that felt good in order to cultivate inner peace. On a macro level, all events in life are neutral, and it's our interpretations and beliefs about those events that give them their emotional charge. I could have chosen to believe my kids would be forever damaged from their relationship with their dad, and that they would develop unhealthy coping mechanisms and relational patterns that would create suffering for them. I clung to that interpretation for a long time, and it felt horrible and caused me ongoing suffering. When I shifted my interpretation, I felt much better, and it allowed me to continue navigating my co-parenting with Chris while maintaining peace within myself.

When I see my kids as learning lessons from their dad that will make them stronger and equip them for the callings that they have in their hearts, I am able to access hope for their future. It allows me to be a better parent because I'm more at peace. I have more love for Chris, and now I'm projecting a vision of a positive future onto my children rather than a negative one.

CHAPTER SEVEN LESSONS:

- For any woman who is in a relationship that is abusive or toxic, you must listen to your own inner voice and not to anyone else around you. If you know in your heart that you need to leave, then that is what you must do, no matter what anyone else says, even if they are in a position of leadership over you.

- You are not your thoughts. You are not your mind. You are not your body. You are divine consciousness, having a human experience.

- Your soul—your consciousness/awareness—is never born and will never die

- Nothing and no one's opinion or interpretation of you has any bearing on who you actually are.

- It is up to you to create interpretations of your life that feel good to think about. By creating positive interpretations, you are raising your energetic vibration, which will attract more of that higher vibration energy into your life.

CHAPTER 8
SELF-LOVE

"By God, when you see your beauty,
you will be the idol of yourself."
—Rumi

I worked with a client named Brittany, who experienced severe abandonment by her parents as a young girl. Due to these early experiences, she developed the beliefs that she didn't deserve love and that she wasn't worthy of someone being there for her. She internalized these beliefs about herself, and as an adult, she manifested a relationship that was reflective of them.

Lesson: *Our relationships are a reflection of what we believe we are worthy of.*

Brittany had attracted a partner who was emotionally and covertly abusive. He would guilt-trip her when she did things alone with her girlfriends, give her the silent treatment for multiple days when she did something that upset him, and shame her for wanting to have her own career and make choices independent of him. Because she was carrying the subconscious beliefs that she wasn't worthy and that the people that she loved the most would leave her, she couldn't see that she was in an unhealthy dynamic. She felt guilty about not wanting to be in the relationship, and she couldn't bring herself to leave him because she thought that leaving him would be selfish.

Over the course of our sessions together, she was able to see how she had created her beliefs of unworthiness through the challenging experiences that she had endured in her childhood. She was able to adopt the new belief that she was worthy of love and that she was worthy of being with a partner who would accept and support her for who she was. She realized that she no longer wanted to be in a relationship in which she wasn't free to be herself.

In our early lives, we all develop a whole swarm of subconscious beliefs about who we are, what we are capable of, and what we are worthy of having. As adults, until we make it a priority to explore and alter these subconscious beliefs, they will rule our decision-making and our actions. Most of the time, we aren't even aware that these beliefs are driving our lives. A powerful subconscious belief that I became aware of and consciously let go of was the belief that I am a victim. It was very easy for me to step out of my divorce and take on the identity of a victim. Many people get stuck in victim consciousness for years, and they allow it to become an excuse for why they can't be happy.

I had to acknowledge that I was a contributing party to what had happened in my marriage because I had chosen to accept behavior that was unacceptable again and again. I hadn't taken a stand so many times when Chris had exhibited abusive behavior. I had allowed it to happen.

Lesson: *What you permit, you promote.*

By owning up to this and taking responsibility for the part that I played, I gained my power back. I was able to clearly and definitively say that I would no longer accept behavior like that in my life. When you let go of victim consciousness and decide to be the author of your own life, you get to create this beautiful dance of co-creation with the Universe. You can consciously choose the kind of human you want to be and the types of relationships and experiences you desire to have while you remain unattached to specific outcomes and trust that the Universe is allowing it all to unfold perfectly for you in divine timing.

When you choose to be the author of your own story, you're also deciding to let go of other people's stories about you and to be unaffected by what other people think about you. When you get really clear about who you are, it doesn't matter what anyone else thinks about you, and what other people decide to think about you is out of your control anyway. It doesn't have the power to affect you unless you let it. You decide who you want to be, and you no longer allow other people to tell you who you can or can't be or what is or isn't possible for you.

Another aspect of transitioning out of victim consciousness is transitioning from the belief that "this happened *to* me" to the belief that "this happened *for* me." This is a powerful distinction that comes from the belief that everything, on a cosmic level, is happening *for* you—for the highest good of your soul. When you're able to see every challenge in your life as a blessing in the form of a spiritual lesson, you are choosing a much more powerful interpretation of your life than when you believe that you are a victim of your life circumstances.

"Life is simple. Everything happens for you, not to you. Everything happens at exactly the right moment, neither too soon nor too late."
—Byron Katie

Lesson: *Everything can be experienced as a blessing when you see it as the perfect growth opportunity that the Universe has designed for your soul.*

In addition to letting go of the belief that you are a victim, you can also choose to let go of worrying about other people's opinions. You no longer need to feel validated by others because you are sourcing your own validation from *within*—where it has always been. This allows you the freedom to take off your masks and to show up in your authenticity. Two masks that I wore very often before I did this work were "polite girl" and "people pleaser." They were the masks that I had learned to wear to feel safe in my childhood and adolescent years. As I got older, though, I realized that these masks weren't me. By continually choosing to wear them, I had lost sight of who I really was. I had lost my true self to the characters that I was playing out of my deep desire to be loved and accepted.

"Authenticity is a collection of choices that we have to make every day. It's about the choice to show up and be real. The choice to be honest. The choice to let our true selves be seen."
—Brené Brown, *The Gifts of Imperfection*

Every time I accepted something that didn't feel right or didn't express my opinion out of fear of what the reaction might be, I lost more of myself. Ultimately, wearing these masks ended up being dangerous for me because not only did I lose myself in their shadow, but they also played a role in allowing me to accept abusive behavior.

When I attended my emotional intelligence training, I was able to see these masks clearly so that I could consciously decide to stop wearing them. I had been telling myself my whole life that my opinions weren't as valuable as the next person's. However, with this new awareness of my masks, I was able to sit back and ask myself, *Who do I want to be?* If I took away societal expectations, social conditioning, and my perceptions of people's expectations for me, who did I really want to be? I realized that I wanted to be a woman who stood in her strength. I realized that I *do* have something worthwhile to say, and it's okay for me to take up space in this world. This is true for *all* of us.

Lesson: There is space for all of us, and we all matter. We are here on this planet at this exact moment for a reason. God/Goddess/Source doesn't make mistakes.

"You are here to enable the divine purpose of the Universe to unfold. That is how important you are!"
—Eckhart Tolle

When I did some self-exploration in an honest and non-judgmental way, I reconnected to parts of myself that I had tucked away for quite some time. I reconnected to my love of dancing, painting, creating music, getting lost in nature, and being wild and spontaneous! I love to connect deeply with other humans and walk barefoot on the earth. I love to collaborate with and create works of art with other beautiful souls, and I love to swim in the ocean (preferably naked). I reconnected with the importance of self-expression, the importance of practicing those things that make you feel free and that make you feel alive. I had to flip a belief that I used to have about selfishness. I thought that making choices to make yourself happy was selfish, but what I learned is that when you deeply honor and take care of yourself, not only does it feel amazing, but it also enables you to be a brighter light in the world for all those around you.

Lesson: *Taking care of yourself is not selfish. Rather, it empowers you to be a brighter light for those around you. Ultimately, taking care of yourself is in the interest of the highest good for all beings.*

We are all such unique and special expressions of the divine. Our purpose is to fully express and fully share our gifts with the world. When we're wearing masks, withholding our contributions out of fear, or acting in accordance with what we believe others' expectations to be, then we're keeping the people in our orbit from experiencing our brightest light. We're withholding our inner treasures from others and robbing them of the possibility of experiencing them, as well as robbing ourselves of the possibility of experiencing ourselves in our highest expression. What a shame!

However, when we allow ourselves to stand in our truth unapologetically, we are acting as an example and creating an invitation for others to do the same. We are giving those around us the energetic invitation to stand in their sovereignty and truth as well.

Another part of self-expression that I began to explore further was my sexuality. Sexuality is something most people experience guilt and shame around, largely due to the religious principles that are deeply ingrained in most cultures. We are meant to be fully expressed in every way, and sexuality is an important part of this. I had to unlearn the guilt that I had associated with being a sexual being and embrace the beauty of it. I adopted a new belief that when sexuality is expressed with love, honor, and respect, it is nothing but beautiful and certainly not anything to be ashamed of or to feel guilty about.

Ultimately, you get to allow yourself the time and space for whatever expression lights you up, whether it's artistic, physical expression through dance and movement, time in nature, or whatever else calls to you. All of this is a part of you and feeds into your inspiration to be connected to what you're meant to cause and create in this world.

We also get to love and embrace our imperfections. This is something I tell my children a lot. Outside of our true spiritual nature, there is no such thing as perfect. In the human realm, perfection doesn't exist, and yet so many of us are perfectionists who are striving to measure up to unattainable and unrealistic standards. Imagine the peace that can come from simply loving yourself exactly as you are. Love the messiness, the scars, the scoliosis, your horrible cooking, your terrible singing voice, or whatever it is for you! We all have things that we are amazing at and things that greatly challenge us, and that is the beauty of it. We are all needed with our specific color and flavor to contribute to the tapestry that is this human experience.

Learn to have fun with yourself instead of being judgmental and down on yourself. You can celebrate and laugh at yourself as you learn to become the observer of your mind, laughing at how silly it can be, at the millions of judgments that go through your head every day. The mind is a separate entity from you. See it for what it is: just the busy mind running on its hamster wheel. We can observe our thoughts and allow them to pass by without judging them. When we choose not to engage with disempowering thoughts, we will no longer feel the emotions that would otherwise be associated with those energy-depleting thoughts.

Another part of embracing yourself exactly as you are is not taking anything personally. When other people are judgmental, it has nothing to do with you. It has to do with their own judgments of themselves. When a person is happy and at peace with themselves, they have no reason to cast judgment on someone else. It's only when you experience your own self-judgment that you turn judgment toward others.

It is only when you are able to love yourself that you will be able to truly love others. Additionally, it's only when you can love and accept yourself exactly as you are that you will have the capacity to attract the type of relationship that you deeply desire. You can only attract into your life what you believe you are worthy of.

When my client, Brittany, acknowledged that she deserves something better than what she was experiencing with her current partner, she was able to leave her unhealthy relationship and start attracting partners who were a reflection of her new belief, *I am worthy of love*. Until she held the belief that she deserved a loving partner, she couldn't attract a healthy relationship into her life. Learn to love yourself first by practicing radical acceptance of yourself exactly as you are. Remind yourself that you have been doing your very best in each moment on your journey. From this place of self-love, you will be able to love others, and you will be able to attract healthy and fulfilling relationships into your life.

Finally, love your process. It's about who you become on your journey. It was never about the destination. And remember, everything is unfolding perfectly for you in divine timing. You can't do it wrong, and you cannot miss what is meant for you, so relax and enjoy the ride!

CHAPTER EIGHT LESSONS:

- Our relationships are a reflection of what we believe we are worthy of.

- What you permit, you promote.

- Everything can be experienced as a blessing when you see it as the perfect growth opportunity that the Universe has designed for your soul.

- There is space for all of us, and we all matter. We are here on this planet at this exact moment for a reason. God/Goddess/Source doesn't make mistakes.

- Taking care of yourself is not selfish. Rather, it empowers you to be a brighter light for those around you. Ultimately, taking care of yourself is in the interest of the highest good for all beings.

- Love your process. It is about the journey, not the destination. You cannot miss what is meant for you.

CHAPTER 9
BELIEFS ABOUT WORTHINESS AND ABUNDANCE

"Create the highest, grandest vision possible for your life, because you become what you believe."
—Oprah Winfrey

L et's talk a little bit more about beliefs because they are so important! As I mentioned earlier, we have a tendency to take our beliefs as truths without examining them, but in reality, many of the beliefs that we carry are simply not true.

Lesson: *A belief is nothing more than a thought that we think over and over until we believe it to be true.*

There is no absolute truth outside of consciousness awareness (outside of God/Goddess). The beliefs that we consider to be true come from the mind. It's extremely important to be aware of our beliefs so we choose beliefs that are supportive of the lives that we want to create for ourselves. What you believe is driving what you are manifesting into your reality.

Rhonda Byrne boils it down very concisely in *The Greatest Secret*: "Whatever circumstances are appearing in your life currently are being generated by your belief system in your subconscious mind." Once you know this, learning how to observe your thoughts becomes even more important. From the vantage point of an observer of your thoughts, you can begin to notice the chatter of your mind. You can learn to observe it, notice its patterns, and question its assertions.

All of the beliefs in your mind come from outside of you. Many of them were accepted by your mind as truth before you were old enough to reason. They come from your parents, your culture, and your society. Once you reach adulthood, your subconscious mind is filled with beliefs—most of which you did not consciously decide to adopt. Now that you are aware of this, you can take an inquiry of your beliefs one by one and ask if they are, in fact, true for you now.

"It is often beneficial to look at some commonly held beliefs and let go of them right in the beginning, such as 1) We only deserve things through hard work, struggle, sacrifice, and effort; 2) Suffering is beneficial and good for us; 3) We don't get anything for nothing; 4) Things that are very simple aren't worth much."
—Dr. David R. Hawkins,
Letting Go: The Pathway of Surrender

It is especially important to deconstruct limiting beliefs around your self-worth and what you believe you deserve. If you grew up in a household in which someone told you on multiple occasions that you would never amount to anything, you may have internalized this belief for yourself. Similarly, if you had a parent who was fun sometimes but cruel and harsh other times, you likely internalized the belief that the people who love you the most also hurt you the most.

This is not an absolute truth, but if it is a belief that you hold, you will continue to attract relationships into your life that mirror this belief.

Lesson: Sometimes, our beliefs are woven so well into our subconscious minds that we take them to be true without question.

Here are a few ideas to help you uncover beliefs that are getting in your way of reaching your full potential:

1. Work with a coach or therapist to help you uncover beliefs that you have not been able to bring to consciousness on your own.

2. Sit in meditation with the intention of cultivating awareness around any subconscious beliefs that are keeping you from being, doing, or having the things in your life that you desire. You can do this by simply sitting quietly and asking your higher power to reveal to you your limiting beliefs. Be quiet and listen to what comes up. Repeat often.

3. Answer one or more of the following journal questions:
   a. What part of my life feels out of alignment?
   b. What things in my life seem like they are not working?
   c. Where in my life do I feel lost?

Once you have answered the journal questions, ask yourself what belief(s) you would need to be true for you in order to create success/satisfaction in whatever area that you are desiring.

Now your work is to become aligned with the new beliefs that will support you in creating what you desire. In this process, it is crucial to choose beliefs that feel true to you. If you are struggling to believe something that you want to believe, such as, *I am worthy of love*, then you can try starting with something close that feels true, such as *Everyone deserves love* or *Love is available to everyone.*

The next step is to search for evidence that proves your new belief to be true. You would search for evidence that *being loved is possible* by talking to or reading about people who are in healthy, loving relationships. Remember, the more you see of something, the more your brain (reticular activating system) will find examples of it, and the easier it will be for you to believe that it is possible for yourself.

In addition to examining the beliefs that you hold, it is extremely liberating to let go of other people's expectations of you. You get to be intentional about what your desires and values are, independent of the society you live in, your family of origin, and the dominant religion in your culture.

Lesson: *You are a sovereign being, and it is within your power to decide who you want to be, what you want to experience, and the life you want to have.*

It takes courage to ask for what you want independent of what others have said you can or can't have/should or shouldn't do. In fact, I encourage you to take "should" out of your vocabulary altogether! I lived so much of my life trying to fit the mold of what *I believed* others wanted for me. Most of us do this. We make a decision based on what our family wants or what society has modeled for us. But when we do this, it's as if we aren't even living our own lives. We are living out someone else's will, and what is the point of that? They are already living out their lives, so you might as well live yours!

Since beliefs are nothing more than thoughts that we think over and over again, we have the power to change them. So, why wouldn't we? Thanks to neuroscience, we know that we can change the shape of our brains. This is so exciting! When I replaced the belief that I was a shy person, I had to keep thinking, *I am a leader, and what I have to say matters,* over and over again until I had no doubt that it was true. I had to lean into this new thought again and again until a new neural pathway was created that replaced the old neural pathway of *I am shy.* To create these new neural pathways, you must simply become aware of a belief that you currently have that is getting in your way, consciously replace it with a belief that will empower you, seek out proof for your new belief, and continue to repeat the new belief to yourself until it feels absolutely true.

Belief Replacement Breakdown:

1. Identify your limiting belief
2. Replace it with a new belief that resonates as true for you
3. Seek out proof for your new belief
4. Repeat the new belief until it feels unquestionably true
5. Congratulations! You have created a new neural pathway! :)

It is also beneficial to raise your vibration by putting your focus on things that make you happy. An extremely powerful and easy practice is conscious gratitude for all the things you have to appreciate.

Lesson: When you practice being truly grateful for what is in front of you, you shift your entire energy, and you create an atmosphere that's conducive to positive thoughts and positive beliefs.

I have learned to practice gratitude in a very tangible way with my children. As a single mom, I am often in situations that, on the surface, can feel really challenging and frustrating. For example, at bath time neither of my kids are cooperating with me to get into the bath. It's late, I'm tired, and my mind is obsessing over the idea that my kids are going to be fussy and unmanageable the next day if they don't get to bed on time. Meanwhile, my kids are completely joyful, chasing each other around with balloons. In that moment, I can either lean into the frustration and fear of not having control, or I can completely flip my internal script and lean into the beauty of what is unfolding before me. I can open my eyes and see the beauty of these two children, whom I love so dearly, playing joyfully and laughing. When I make this internal shift, I am flooded with gratitude.

Sometimes, I even imagine that I'm visiting the present moment from the future when my kids are adults, and I miss that childlike joy and silliness. I bring myself intensely into the present moment and fixate on the beauty of these laughing children. When I do this, I'm able to access such a deep level of gratitude and love for them. Often, just being in that state naturally leads to them getting in the bath, but if it doesn't, no biggie. I can let it go!

When you focus on the positive, you raise your vibration and attract more of that positive energy to you. What you're grateful for expands. Conversely, if your focus is on the negative, you will attract more experiences of a lower vibration. In other words, whatever vibration you're carrying in your body is drawing to you more experiences of a similar vibration. After twenty years of research, David R. Hawkins, MD, created a chart that shows different emotional states and the vibrational frequencies that they carry. You can acquire a deep understanding of how this works in his book, *The Map of Consciousness Explained.*

Essentially what it points to is that when we're experiencing emotions such as of anger, guilt, or shame, we are vibrating at much lower frequencies and, therefore, drawing people, experiences, and situations of those lower frequencies to us. On the other end of the spectrum, when we experience emotions such as love, joy, acceptance, or surrender, we vibrate at much higher frequencies, and therefore, we draw people, experiences, and situations of those higher frequencies to us.

Lesson: The emotional frequency at which you are vibrating is attracting more thoughts, emotions, and experiences of that same frequency to you.

A very powerful belief that I had to rewire for myself was the belief that if I got something, I was keeping someone else from having that thing. I remember as a little girl being in the grocery store parking lot with my parents. My dad drove a BMW, and I noticed another little girl around my age going to her car with her family. Their car was old and beat up. It was one of the first times as a child that I became aware that my experience wasn't the same as everyone else's. I felt so sad for the other little girl, and I felt guilty that my family had money and hers did not. For a time, I grappled with feeling guilty about everything my family and I could do that others couldn't.

Similarly, when I was pursuing acting in Los Angeles, I remember sitting in audition rooms with many other girls like me, and I would feel bad about the prospect of getting the role and everyone else having to go home without it. I had to let go of feeling guilty for what I had been given and instead accept my gifts and use them to give back to the world and to those around me.

Lesson: There is no lack of resources in the Universe. There is always enough for everyone.

I chose to embrace "abundance mentality," which is the belief that the supplies of the Universe are limitless and therefore there is *always* enough for everyone. I used to hold the belief that it was selfish for me to desire a nice house and plenty of resources to travel and do the things that I desire to do in life. I believed that it wasn't fair for me to have those things if other people didn't have them.

When you create from a place of abundance, you're creating from a paradigm of win-win instead of win-lose. I think a lot of healers and teachers navigate guilt around wanting to earn money for helping people. There are a lot of negative beliefs out there about money, such as people with money are greedy or people with money exploit other people, and sometimes those things are true. On the other hand, there are many people with money who are doing amazing things to give back to our world. I've learned that you can only be fully expressed in whatever it is that you're trying to create in the world when you have the resources to create those things. You can only help others if you are able to take care of yourself first.

If your desire is to go out and speak on stages for people, you have to be able to support yourself to do that. If you want to write a book, or if you want to create art or music, you must have the resources to support yourself in pursuing these beautiful dreams. We live in a world that requires us to have money, and if all of our efforts are going just toward paying our rent, bills, etc., then we can't be fully expressed in whatever it is that we're meant to create. Embracing the beliefs that you deserve to make money, there's enough for everyone, and desiring to be well cared for is not a selfish desire will empower you to create the abundance that will empower you to share your gifts. You fully expressing your gifts to the world is in the highest and best interest of all beings. If the conscious thinkers and peacemakers of the world had more money, think of all the great things they could create for humanity!

If you have a conversation about money that keeps you from believing that you deserve to have it, I encourage you to turn that belief around and know that you are worthy of being fully compensated for your gifts and that there is truly enough for everyone.

Shifting my beliefs around what I deserved and who I was capable of being had a huge impact on my life. I no longer feel guilty for the gifts that I have, and I no longer believe that I cannot create what is in my heart to create. Only when you decide to be the author of your own life and step into your full power to share your gifts with the world will you allow yourself to shine at your fullest capacity. Only then will the world be able to experience the enormous love and light that you have to give!

CHAPTER NINE LESSONS:

- A belief is nothing more than a thought that we think over and over until we believe it to be true.

- Sometimes, our beliefs are woven so well into our subconscious minds that we take them to be true without question.

- You are a sovereign being, and it is within your power to decide who you want to be, what you want to experience, and the life you want to have.

- When you practice being truly grateful for what is in front of you, you shift your entire energy, and you create an atmosphere that's conducive to positive thoughts and positive beliefs.

- The emotional frequency at which you are vibrating is attracting more thoughts, emotions, and experiences of that same frequency to you.

- There is no lack of resources in the Universe. There is always enough for everyone.

RELATIONSHIPS: OUR BEST TEACHERS

"Relationships are constantly challenging, constantly calling you to create, express, and experience higher and higher aspects of yourself, grander and grander visions of yourself, ever more magnificent versions of yourself. Nowhere can you do this more immediately, impactfully, and immaculately than in relationships. In fact, without relationships, you cannot do it at all. Once you clearly understand this, once you deeply grasp it, then you intuitively bless each and every experience, all human encounters, and especially the personal human relationships, where you see them as constructive in the highest sense. You see that they can be used, must be used, are being used, whether you want them to or not, to construct who you really are.
—Neale Donald Walsch,
Conversations with God: An Uncommon Dialogue

A n enormous lesson that I've learned on my journey is that striving to change other human beings only brings suffering to you and to them. We cannot change others. I spent a lot of time in my marriage trying to change Chris, trying to take away his anger. I sent him countless links to podcasts and articles about controlling anger and encouraged him to join men's groups or seek a male counselor, just hoping that it would take away his temper and the pain that I felt because of it.

One of the greatest gifts that you can give someone is to fully accept, love, and embrace them exactly as they are. However, accepting someone for who they are doesn't mean that you accept unacceptable behavior from them. Creating healthy boundaries is essential to taking care of your own healthy mental space. You can love someone and choose to leave him. You can accept someone for who they are and still choose not to spend time with him. You can choose to love him from afar while choosing simultaneously to protect your own inner peace. Creating boundaries creates the highest and best outcome for all involved, even if the other person is resistant to them.

Lesson: *Sometimes, leaving people is the most loving thing that you can do for them. This is because staying is allowing them to treat you in a way that they know deep down is not okay, and even though they chose to engage in that behavior, they are suffering too (because only someone who is suffering would treat someone else that poorly). By leaving them, you are giving them an opportunity to do work on themselves and to become a better person through the experience of looking honestly at the role that they played in the dissolution of the relationship.*

Focusing on the negative aspects that you experience with someone in a relationship will only intensify your experience of those negative qualities. As I mentioned before, whatever you put your focus on is what will expand in your experience. So, rather than focusing on the things that you don't like about someone, focus on the things that you do like. When you are easily triggered by someone, finding qualities about him or her that you appreciate can seem *very* challenging at first, but when you look with genuine curiosity, there is always something that you can find to appreciate about a person, even if it is simply that he or she is showing you how not to be or illustrating how blessed you are to be able to make different choices than him or her.

This refocusing or reframing of what you put your attention on will also drastically improve your relationship with your children if you're a parent. It's easy to see the things that frustrate us in our children, the things that we wish were different, or the things that make us worry about them. I have found that by focusing on the things I love about my children and on their strengths, I've cultivated more peace as a parent and so much more love for my children. This can be illustrated through the way that I reframed the story that I was telling myself about my son, Robert.

Robert is an absolute *tour de force*. I've never met anyone with his energy or level of passion. He's neurodivergent and a brilliant genius. As a seven-year-old, he could solve a Rubik's cube in under thirty seconds. His energy can be explosive, like a time bomb that may go off inside the house at any point if he gets bored or dysregulated. I have spent many hours worrying about him because he has anger outbursts that can be scary for me and his little sister.

This is an extremely difficult thing to navigate as a parent, not only because it's unpleasant but because I've worried about the implications of his lack of impulse control on his future. Once I was able to see that I was leaning into this worry excessively, I realized that I had to change the story that I was telling myself about him. I had to change the story into one that would be supportive of the future that I desired for him. So, rather than seeing his energy and his anger outbursts as a constant source of worry, I reframed them as his superpower.

Not that losing your temper is a superpower, but being a human being with so much energy and so much passion, when cultivated properly, can create amazing things, and this is the vision of the future that I now hold for him. That energy, that force that he has, is something exquisite and unique, and, if geared in a positive direction, it can result in miraculous things for and through him. When I lean into this belief, I feel peace, and I'm also able to walk away from his outbursts with a sense of acceptance rather than a sense of dread and defeat.

It's really hard as a parent to not worry about your children. But worry does nothing but create harm to ourselves. Remember that what you focus on, you see more of. I've learned that my children are perfect as they are. Their stories are unfolding on their own divine timelines that are ultimately outside of my control.

It is comforting to me that many of the enlightened sages and spiritual teachers experienced great difficulty in their early lives. It was these childhoods that plunged them into the depths of their spiritual work. What may be perceived in the present moment as a disadvantage may turn out to be your greatest gift because it may put you on a life path that you would have otherwise not found for yourself. In other words, though it seems extremely counterintuitive, suffering can be the greatest gift that a human can be given.

I've also learned that our kids aren't here to be a source of pleasure for us, even though they often are. That's not their purpose. They are not here to realize our dreams for them. They are here to realize their own dreams for themselves and to walk out the spiritual lessons that their souls require in this lifetime. They are here to live out their own divine purpose, and we, as parents, are ultimately here to accept them exactly as they are and to love and encourage them. I personally have leaned into a deep gratitude for both of my children, exactly as they are, and I delight in them daily.

"When there is no emotional investment in trying to force things
to be the way we want them, then they are
free to move and resolve themselves."
—Kalyani Lawry

I'd also like to share a reframing that supported me in my romantic relationships. The consensus in our culture is that a relationship is a success if people stay together and a failure when people break up. Additionally, a relationship is considered to be good when everything is peaceful and bad when people are in conflict. What I've learned, though, is that it is much more nuanced than this. There is a higher purpose to relationships than simply lasting.

The purpose of a relationship, outside of giving and receiving love, is to learn more about yourself and to teach the other more about him or herself. It is to decide what parts of you that you want to explore deeper and to offer the same opportunity to your partner. I think one of the most powerful things a romantic relationship can offer to a person is a calling forth of those parts of you that you wish to expand upon and express. Relationships are not necessarily meant to last forever. Some relationships are only present for a season of learning, and then they complete their purpose. We are not meant to cling to them but rather to love them completely for as long as they are there and allow them to go if and when they need to go.

There can only be one purpose for relationships and for all of life:
to be and decide who you really are.
—Neale Donald Walsch

From this perspective, we can explore the notion that there is no bad relationship because all relationships are simply invitations for us to cultivate a deeper understanding and expression of our true selves. Every person in your life can be a spiritual teacher. When I was able to look at Chris, not as the villain in my story, but as a spiritual teacher, I was actually able to cultivate deep love and appreciation for him. I have learned so many spiritual lessons from interacting with him. He's taught me how to stand in my power, how to set energetic and emotional boundaries, and how to remain neutral in situations that would have otherwise caused suffering.

Lesson: *Every relationship in your life is an opportunity to go deeper and learn more about your authentic self.*

When you look at any relationship from the vantage point of what is available to learn, you can cultivate gratitude for it, no matter how tumultuous it is. Once I made this mental shift in regard to Chris, I was able to transform the hatred that I had toward him into love, compassion, and even appreciation. On a cosmic level, I know that our souls made a contract to teach and learn from each other in this lifetime. To me, this is a beautiful expression of the deepest kind of love.

Lesson: *Who you perceive to be your greatest enemy or the most difficult person in your life may be one of your most powerful spiritual teachers if you can start to shift your perspective around him/her.*

I no longer have deep anger toward Chris. I no longer have hatred toward myself for choosing him as the father of my children. I no longer have regret for having married him or having had children with him because I accept that it's all part of my divine plan. The same is true for your parents, siblings, partners, and children. So many of my clients talk about how they wish their relationship with their mom, dad, sister, or brother was different. They deeply wish that their mom or dad could show up in this way or that so that they could feel loved and understood. I think this is something that most people can identify with. We internalize the belief that other people have perfect families, and that we are the exception in our family's dysfunction. In my experience, dysfunction is the norm, so none of us are alone in that.

What are your relationships with your parents teaching you about you? You can shift from your desire to get something from them to being curious about what it is that you can learn about yourself and who you want to be in the world through your experience of that relationship. You can also choose to love them exactly as they are. If they are a toxic person, then you can choose to love them from afar. Loving someone does not mean that you abandon your boundaries to bend to their will. Loving someone simply means that you accept them as they are while simultaneously taking care of your own needs.

I recently listened to a neuroscientist named James Cooke speak on *The Weekend University* podcast. He explained that each of us, had we had the same exact experience as any other human, would be exactly like them. We would make the same choices they make and act in the same ways that they act. This supports the idea expressed earlier that each of us is doing the very best we can in every moment based on our DNA and everything we have experienced thus far in our lives. The people in our lives are unable to show up in any other way than in the way that they are. Knowing this can cultivate a great amount of compassion for those people who trigger us.

One of my coaching mentors explained how, for the longest time, she resisted who her mom was. It was a continual source of suffering for her until, eventually, after much self-development work, she decided to lean into full acceptance of who her mom was. Whenever her mom would engage in certain behaviors that used to trigger her and make her angry, she started saying, "Of course, she's doing that because that's what she does," or "There goes Mom being Mom."

Another one of my coaches put it this way: "You can't go to a maple tree and expect to get milk." If you think about it, it's insane to expect something different from a person other than who they are. It only creates suffering and frustration for you and for them. Again, you cannot change people, so why create suffering for all involved by wishing they were different or resisting who they are?

One of the most important things I can do for my clients is to hold a safe and loving space of complete acceptance for them. That, in and of itself, is healing for people. Most people don't have many people (if any) in their lives who love and accept them wholeheartedly without any expectation of them acting or being a certain way.

Lesson: Letting go of your expectations for the people in your life and choosing to love them exactly as they are will create peace for you and for them.

At the end of the day, our relationships are here to teach us more about who we are and who we desire to be in the world. No relationship is a waste of time. No relationship or marriage that ends is a failure in the highest sense because there is always learning available to you from your experience in that relationship. When you begin to appreciate your relationships for what they are teaching you and you choose to love and accept each person in your life exactly as they are, your perspective on relationships will transform into one in which you see that failure isn't even possible. It is all just learning.

Perfect love casts out fear. Where there is love, there are no demands,
no expectations, no dependency. I do not demand that you make me
happy; my happiness does not lie in you. If you were to leave me,
I will not feel sorry for myself; I enjoy your company
immensely, but I do not cling.
—Anthony de Mello,
Awareness: The Perils and Opportunities of Reality

CHAPTER TEN LESSONS:

- Sometimes, leaving people is the most loving thing that you can do for them. This is because staying is allowing them to treat you in a way that they know deep down is not okay, and even though they chose to engage in that behavior, they are suffering too (because only someone who is suffering would treat someone else that poorly). By leaving them, you are giving them an opportunity to do work on themselves and become a better person through the experience of looking honestly at the role that they played in the dissolution of the relationship.

- Every relationship in your life is an opportunity to go deeper and learn more about your authentic self.

- Who you perceive to be your greatest enemy or the most difficult person in your life may be one of your most powerful spiritual teachers if you can start to shift your perspective around him or her.

- Letting go of your expectations for the people in your life and choosing to love them exactly as they are will create peace for you and for them.

CHAPTER 11
ALL IS WELL

"There is only one purpose in all of life, and that is for you and all that lives to experience fullest glory. You can choose to be a person who has resulted from what has happened or from what you've chosen to be and do about what has happened."
—Neale Donald Walsch

T he biggest lesson that I've learned in everything that I've studied is that you can access deep peace and lasting joy through the simple act of loving and accepting what is. If you think about it, any time you resist what is, you're creating suffering for yourself. When you say *no* to what is in front of you, you experience suffering. When you accept what is in front of you, you experience peace. It is really as simple as that, though it takes practice for this to become your way of being.

"I'm a lover of what is, not because I'm a spiritual person, but because it hurts when I argue with reality."
—Byron Kaite, *Loving What Is*

When you learn to accept the things in your life that you can't change, from the small things like traffic jams to the big things like custody agreements, you will experience a higher level of peace. On a broad spiritual level, everything is as it should be, and all is well because we are only in our human bodies for a time, and when we die, we shed our bodies and wake up to the divine nature that we have always been. We return to our true nature, which is effortless being.

Mystics throughout time have agreed that even as we see the violence, chaos, and suffering in the world, on a Divine Consciousness level, all is well and will always be well. If that consciousness was never created and can never be destroyed, and we are manifestations of that Divine Consciousness, then the truest essence of all of us is eternal and unchanging. Whatever harm comes to us on this earthly plane, our souls remain immaculate and untarnished. Knowing this allows you to have peace and allows you to surrender and trust that the universe has your back in everything at all times. Goddess is carrying you, and everything is unfolding perfectly for you in divine timing, even when it really doesn't seem like it!

When you see everyone and every sentient being in the world as an extension of the same consciousness that you are, it will look entirely different from what it looked like when you experienced other beings as being separate from you. You have the capacity to love and identify with every person and living being on the planet. When you move from the perspective that we're all connected—that we're all one, it's impossible to desire to do harm to anyone or anything because, in essence, you are doing harm to yourself.

As I mentioned earlier, one of the greatest gifts that we can give to another human is to fully love and accept them exactly as they are. This starts with fully loving and accepting ourselves exactly as we are. Most of us are continually striving to create external comforts for ourselves, such as a better house, car, and clothes. However, the work that reaps true joy is the inner work. The real work is taking the time to sit in stillness. The Bible says, "Be still and know that I am God" (Psalm 46:10). Another way to interpret this is: Be still and sit with the divine eternal presence that is inside of all of us and therefore always available to us.

When we sit in silence and connect with consciousness awareness, we can disengage from our chattering mind. This is where peace starts, and this is how we begin to heal ourselves and the world. Multiple studies have shown that when large groups of people meditate together, the crime rates in their cities go down. When Mother Teresa was asked, "What can you do to promote world peace?" her answer was, "Go home and love your family." Loving your family starts with loving yourself, and loving yourself starts with accepting yourself exactly as you are. Consciousness Awareness/Love is all there was, all there is, and all there ever will be. When you're able to connect with that love, you see that you are perfect, whole, and complete exactly as you are, and so is everyone else.

All of our energy is connected, and everything we do matters. Have you ever experienced harboring a negative feeling toward someone and then felt as though that person reacted to your negative feeling, even though you didn't say anything or act any differently? It's as if they knew what you were thinking and feeling about them. This is because your energy is tangibly felt on a vibrational level. What you think and feel projects out into the world. It matters. It is a powerful practice to let go of negative feelings that you harbor toward anyone because by harboring those negative feelings, you're creating an energetic heaviness within yourself that actually hinders your own growth and evolution.

I used to think that the way I could be a force for change in the world was to go out and fight against the things that I thought were wrong. There was a time when I wanted to fight against the broken American family court system, but then I learned that what you resist persists and that what you give energy to expands. The most effective way that you can change the world for the better is to change yourself from within. It is to connect to that inner peace and love that is ever present within you. Change in the world will happen on its own when more individuals do the work to change themselves. You're creating an energy of love that is being pushed out from you into the universe for all of eternity.

MY INVITATIONS TO YOU:

- Learn to see the challenges in your life as blessings and learning opportunities to step fully into the human that you are meant to be.

- Forgive yourself and others fully for past hurts—we are all doing our best with what we have experienced and been given. Remember, forgiveness frees YOU!

- Learn to see the relationships in your life that may, on the exterior, seem challenging as invitations to step into your truest form of self-expression.

- Understand that it is all happening *for* you, not *to* you.

- Understand that we are all one.

- Understand that on a cosmic level, everything is perfect, all is well, and everything is unfolding for you exactly as it should and in divine timing.

- Know that you don't have to fight for change, but rather that change will happen on its own when you live from the vantage point of the observer (consciousness awareness) and trust the Universe.

- Know and embody these things, and you will have peace and love in your life toward yourself and toward everyone in our beautiful world.

CONCLUSION

You are a unique expression of Divine Consciousness, and as such, you are perfect, whole, and complete exactly as you are. I want this reminder to empower you to lean into deep love and appreciation for yourself. *You are amazing*! I hope you know in your heart that everything in your life is unfolding perfectly in divine timing for your highest good. Whatever difficulties you've traversed or are currently traversing—divorce, abuse, poverty, violence—happened *for* you, for your soul's spiritual evolution, and despite whatever happened in your past, you still get to be the author of your story because you are the only one who can choose an empowering interpretation that will support you in creating the future that you desire.

If you resist what life is presenting to you, you will only create suffering, but when you let go of resistance to what is and accept and embrace what is, the magic of the Universe will unfold within you and all around you. Remember that you are in control of your experience because you are the only one who has the power to decide what thoughts you choose to believe.

Finally, I want you to know that you're never alone. We are all eternally connected, and you can always access the deepest of loves from within yourself because, at your core, love is all you have ever been and all you will ever be.

If you are currently navigating a difficult season or if you desire support implementing any of the practices in this book, feel free to reach out. I am honored to serve. www.ashleylaneadams.com

In deepest gratitude and with much love,

Ashley

Click above to watch the Suffering to Surrender supplemental videos.

SUGGESTED READING

- *Conversations with God: An Uncommon Dialog* by Neale Donald Walsch
- *Letting Go: The Pathway of Surrender* by David R. Hawkins
- *Loving What Is* by Byron Kaite
- *Pussy* by Regina Thomashauer
- *The Four Agreements* by don Miguel Ruiz
- *The Greatest Secret* by Rhonda Burne
- *The Power of Now* by Eckart Tolle
- *The Sedona Method* by Hale Dwoskin
- *The Surrender Experiment* by Michael A Singer
- *The Map of Consciousness Explained* by David R Hawkins

THANK YOU FOR READING MY BOOK!

Just to say thanks for buying and reading my book,
I would like to give you a free bonus gift:
A meditation for you to cultivate inner peace!
In gratitude,
Ashley

Scan the QR code to access your free gift:

I appreciate your interest in my book and value your feedback, as it helps me improve future versions of this book. I would appreciate it if you could leave your invaluable review on Amazon.com with your feedback.
Thank you!